DONAL SKEHAN
HOMECOOKED

DONAL SKEHAN
HOMECOOKED

HarperCollins*Publishers*

CONTENTS

INTRODUCTION

There is nothing I love more than a good home-cooked meal. For me, the atmosphere and sentiment goes beyond anything you could have eating out and the idea of sharing food with family and friends is what home cooking is all about.

This book is a collection of 100 tasty and achievable recipes, which I hope are going to encourage people to get into the kitchen and get cooking. The recipes I love to write are ones that I just know will be used time and time again, and in this book I've combined family favourites with new and exciting recipes, which I'm so excited to add to my collection.

Inspiration for the recipes I write come mainly from my travels in Ireland and abroad. I always carry a notebook with me to write down any new and exciting ingredients I might come across or memorable meals that I just have to share. Recipes like Crusty Croque Madam from my summers in Paris and my Griddled Beef & Mint Salad from a recent trip to Vietnam are great weekday meals and they are both exciting and easy to prepare.

Every good home cook knows there are many different types of meals that have to fit into busy lifestyles and so the recipes in this book are broken up into chapters based around the different types of meals that I like to cook throughout the year.

From everyday dinners like Maple Pork Chops with Griddled Baby Gem Lettuce or Chilli & Lemongrass Chicken for snappy weekday meals, to food to share with friends like my Jerk Chicken with Mango Salsa and Mexican Fish Tacos and, of course, big dinners like Roast Beef with Salsa Verde and Sticky Pork with Crackling & an Apple & Ginger Sauce for those family Sunday lunches with all the trimmings. Cooking at home is a great way to stay healthy with the right sort of dishes and in my fast and healthy chapter, I've put together some of my favourite healthy dishes, which certainly aren't lacking on the flavour front. Lime & Coconut Chicken, Blackened Salmon with Green Goddess Avocado Salad and Butterflied Rosemary Chicken with Romesco Sauce certainly won't leave you hungry.

For colder darker days there is a whole chapter on comfort food that is filled with the type of recipes that will bring some warmth when you need it most. Braised Shoulder of Lamb, Three-cheese Lasagne, Howth Head Seafood Chowder and Boeuf Bourginon tick all the boxes.

Weekends are covered, too, and there are lots of recipe ideas for lazy Saturday and Sunday mornings when breakfast becomes brunch. Caramelised Banana Pancakes, Eggs Benedict and Brioche French Toast with Berries & Chocolate – what a way to wake up!

When I was growing up, my favourite recipes to make were sweet, so I couldn't write a book without satisfying my sweet tooth and I've included two delectably delicious chapters full of desserts, sweet treats and baking recipes. Classics like the my Profiterole Mountain dripping with chocolate sauce and a super sweet Lemon Meringue Pie oozing with lemon curd sit quite happily beside my childhood favourites, which I've given a bit of a makeover to, like my Mikado Coconut Cream Cake and Salted Caramel Biscuits.

I hope that this book provides you with lots of inspiration for cooking at home and that you will be reaching for it again and again, splattered, dog-eared and full of wonderful food memories.

Happy Cooking!

EVERYDAY DINNER

Maple Pork Chops with Griddled Baby Gem Lettuce 12/ Chilli & Lemongrass Chicken 14/ Prosciutto-wrapped Cheesy Chicken with Wild Mushroom Sauce 16/ Chilli & Tomato Crab Pasta 18/ Thai Rice Noodle Salad 20/ Braised Crispy Chicken Thighs with Spring Onions, Baby Gem & Peas 21/ Beer Batter Fish with Pea Mash & Rosti Potato Cakes 22/ Sole Meunière 24/ Flavour Bomb Salad 25/ Spicy Seafood Paella 26/ Pasta alla Norma 28

Sweet maple syrup, tangy vinegar and salty soy sauce with a kick of freshness from coriander really make for an extra special pork chop in this recipe. I particularly love serving them with griddled Baby Gem lettuce (a trick I picked up in America), which turns this humble salad green into something smoky, meaty and fresh.

MAPLE PORK CHOPS WITH GRIDDLED BABY GEM LETTUCE

SERVES 4

1 tbsp butter

1 tbsp rapeseed oil, plus extra for brushing

4 large pork loin chops on the bone, 2.5cm thick

Sea salt and ground black pepper

1 small red onion, peeled and finely sliced

1 tbsp apple cider vinegar

4 tbsp maple syrup

1 tbsp light soy sauce

4 tbsp apple juice

4 Baby Gem lettuce, cut in half lengthways

Large handful of coriander leaves, roughly chopped, plus extra to garnish

5 spring onions, trimmed and finely sliced, to garnish

Preheat the oven to 190°C (375°F), Gas Mark 5.

Melt the butter with the oil in a large ovenproof frying pan over a high heat. Pat the pork chops dry with a little kitchen paper and season with sea salt and ground black pepper. Add the chops to the pan and brown on both sides.

When the meat has a good colour, add the onion and fry for about 30 seconds. Then pour in the vinegar, maple syrup, soy sauce and apple juice and heat until the sauce is bubbling. Baste the meat well with the sauce and then place the pan in the oven on the middle shelf and cook for 10 minutes.

While the pork chops are cooking, place a large griddle pan over a high heat and brush the lettuce halves all over with a little of the oil, and season with sea salt and ground black pepper. Place the lettuce halves onto the griddle and cook for about 2 minutes on either side until they have nice deep char marks but still hold their shape. Remove from the heat and set aside.

When the chops are cooked, transfer to a warmed plate and reduce the sauce over a medium heat for a few minutes until slightly thickened. Add the coriander and stir through, then add the chops and the Baby Gem and coat generously in the sauce.

Serve the chops on warmed plates with the charred Baby Gem and scatter with spring onions and a little extra coriander.

This is a wonderfully fragrant dish that is very easy to prepare. I use chicken thighs here as they have more flavour, but you can easily use chicken breasts instead. The paste made for the sauce can also be used with beef or pork.

CHILLI & LEMONGRASS CHICKEN

SERVES 2

2 lemongrass stalks, finely chopped

1 red chilli, deseeded and finely chopped

2 garlic cloves, peeled and finely chopped

1 tbsp Thai fish sauce (Nam Pla)

350g chicken thigh meat, cut into
 bite-sized chunks

1 tbsp sunflower oil

1 tbsp curry powder

100ml chicken stock

1 tbsp caster sugar

Small handful of mint, basil and
 coriander leaves, to garnish

In a bowl, combine the lemongrass, chilli, garlic and fish sauce. Place the chicken meat into another bowl and add half the lemongrass mix, reserving the rest. Cover and place in the fridge to marinate for at least 20 minutes.

Heat the oil in a wok or a large non-stick frying pan over a high heat. Add the reserved lemongrass mixture, then add the curry powder and stir-fry for about 1 minute until fragrant. Then add the marinated chicken and stir-fry for 4–5 minutes until the pieces have a nice colour on all sides.

Pour the chicken stock into the pan and stir in the sugar. Simmer for a few minutes until the stock has reduced and you are left with a thick sauce. Serve with steamed rice and garnish with the herbs.

This is a warm and comforting supper that doesn't take too much time to prepare. You can serve it with either steamed rice or a simply dressed salad, but the two key components are the crisp prosciutto-wrapped chicken oozing with cheese and rich and creamy mushroom sauce. You won't be able to say no!

PROSCIUTTO-WRAPPED CHEESY CHICKEN WITH WILD MUSHROOM SAUCE

SERVES 4

100g Gruyère cheese, finely grated
100g frozen spinach, thawed, squeezed of excess liquid and finely chopped
4 chicken breasts
8 slices of prosciutto
1 tbsp olive oil

FOR THE MUSHROOM SAUCE

50g dried mushrooms
200ml chicken stock
1 tbsp butter
1 onion, peeled and finely sliced
100g mixed fresh mushrooms, sliced
1 garlic clove, peeled and finely chopped
75ml white wine
125ml single cream
Sea salt and ground black pepper
Small handful of flat-leaf parsley, to garnish

Preheat the oven to 200°C (400°F), Gas Mark 6. For the mushroom sauce, soak the dried mushrooms in a bowl with the chicken stock.

To stuff the chicken, mix together the grated cheese and chopped spinach in a bowl. Lay the chicken breasts on a chopping board and, using a sharp knife, slice horizontally to create a pocket. Stuff each pocket with the cheese and spinach mix. Wrap two slices of prosciutto around each chicken breast.

Heat the oil in a a large frying pan over a high heat. Add the chicken breasts and fry all over until they are crisp and golden. Transfer the breasts to a roasting tin and cook on the middle shelf in the oven for about 10 minutes until the prosciutto is crispy and the chicken is cooked through.

Meanwhile, make the mushroom sauce. Add the butter to the pan and place it back on a medium heat. Fry the onion and fresh mushrooms for about 6 minutes until tender. Then add the garlic and fry for another 2 minutes. Pour in the soaked dried mushrooms together with the chicken stock and add the white wine. Bring the sauce to the boil, then reduce the heat and simmer for 2–3 minutes until slightly thickened. Remove the pan from the heat and stir in the cream. Season with sea salt and ground black pepper to taste.

Sprinkle the cooked chicken breast with parsley and serve with the mushroom sauce and some rice, pasta or salad leaves.

I love taking one ingredient and really making it the star of the dish. In this recipe, crab hits the big time! Paired with the heat of chilli and the freshness of lemon juice and zest, it makes a pretty incredible pasta dish. You can buy crab meat quite easily nowadays and for a speedy supper it does save you the hassle of buying a crab, cooking it and then tearing out its insides. Hey, I'm all for shortcuts if you can take them!

CHILLI & TOMATO CRAB PASTA

SERVES 4

Sea salt

300g spaghetti or linguine

3 tbsp olive oil

3 garlic cloves, peeled and finely chopped

1 tsp dried chilli flakes

2 x 400g tins of chopped tomatoes

75ml white wine

150g cooked white crab meat

3 tbsp single cream

Grated zest and juice of 1 lemon

1 heaped tbsp capers, drained and rinsed

Good handful of flat-leaf parsley, chopped, to garnish

Extra virgin olive oil, to drizzle

Bring a large pot of water to the boil over a high heat. Season with salt and pop in the pasta. Cook as instructed on the packet until al dente and then drain.

While the pasta is cooking, heat the oil in a non-stick frying pan over a medium heat. Add the garlic and chilli flakes and fry for about 2 minutes, then add the tomatoes and wine and bring to a steady simmer. Cook for 10 minutes and then stir through the crab meat, cream, lemon zest and juice and capers. Allow the sauce to bubble away for 2–3 minutes and then tumble in the pasta.

Mix through until the pasta is coated and serve in generous mounds on warmed plates, garnishing with the parsley and a drizzle of extra virgin olive oil.

Anyone who has ever travelled to Thailand will remember the wonderful balance of flavours from sweet to salty and spicy to smoky. I like to think this salad captures all this. There are so many wonderful textures and flavours from the roasted nuts, fresh crunchiness from the vegetables and then super sweet heat from the chilli and ginger dressing. This makes a really exciting midweek dinner.

THAI RICE NOODLE SALAD

SERVES 4

250g rice vermicelli noodles

3 Baby Gem lettuce, leaves separated

2 large carrots, peeled and finely sliced

½ cucumber, peeled lengthways
  into ribbons

6 spring onions, trimmed and finely
  sliced

60g salted peanuts, roughly chopped

Large handful of coriander leaves

Large handful of mint leaves

Large handful of basil leaves

FOR THE CHILLI AND GINGER DRESSING

Juice of 1 lime

1 tbsp caster sugar

1 tbsp light soy sauce

2 tbsp Thai fish sauce (Nam Pla)

1 red chilli, deseeded and finely sliced

1 thumb-sized piece of fresh ginger,
  peeled and finely grated

Soak the noodles in a bowl of boiling water according to the packet's instructions until they are tender. Drain the noodles, rinse under cold water and set aside.

For the dressing, whisk together the lime juice and caster sugar in a large mixing bowl until it has dissolved. Add the soy sauce, fish sauce, chilli and ginger and mix through. Then add the noodles, vegetables, peanuts and fresh herbs. Toss to combine and then serve.

True comfort food in a matter of minutes; that's what this dish is all about. Crispy chicken in a white wine sauce with wonderful braised greens and a pop of zesty citrus freshness, it really doesn't get better than that for a speedy midweek supper.

BRAISED CRISPY CHICKEN THIGHS WITH SPRING ONIONS, BABY GEM & PEAS

SERVES 4

1 tbsp olive oil

100g smoked streaky bacon, roughly chopped

6–8 boneless chicken thighs with skin on

1 tbsp butter

Grated zest of 1 lemon

75ml white wine

A few thyme sprigs

50ml chicken stock

200g frozen peas

6 spring onions, trimmed and sliced in half

4 Baby Gem lettuce, sliced in half

Heat the oil in a large high-sided frying pan over a high heat. Add the bacon and fry until crisp. Then add the chicken thighs and fry on each side until they are also golden and crisp. Add the butter and allow it to foam, then stir in the lemon zest and fry it in the butter.

Pour in the wine and allow to sizzle for about 30 seconds before adding the thyme sprigs and chicken stock. Add the peas to the liquid and then nuzzle in the spring onions and Baby Gem lettuce. Cover with a lid and cook for about 10 minutes until the chicken is cooked through. Serve straight away as it is or with a little rice to stretch the meal.

This has to be one of my absolute favourite dinners. It's basically fish and chips, but with a great twist using crispy rosti potato cakes instead of the more laborious chip. I shallow fry my goujons rather than using a deep fat fryer, with oil I keep in a bottle specifically for this purpose. When you're done and the oil is cold, just fill the bottle up to use again next time.

BEER BATTER FISH WITH PEA MASH & ROSTI POTATO CAKES

SERVES 4

Sunflower or rapeseed oil, for frying

500g skinless fish fillets, such as haddock, cod or hake, cut into goujon-sized pieces

3–4 tbsp plain flour, plus 75g for the batter

200ml cold beer

Lemon wedges, to serve

FOR THE ROSTI POTATO CAKES

600g waxy potatoes, peeled

1 tbsp rapeseed oil

Sea salt and ground black pepper

1 tbsp butter

FOR THE PEA MASH

1 tbsp butter

200g frozen peas

1 tbsp extra virgin olive oil

Good handful of mint leaves

Preheat the oven to 180°C (350°F), Gas Mark 4.

To make the rosti potato cakes, grate the potato into a clean dry tea towel. Gather the towel around the potato and form a small ball. Squeeze it over the sink to remove the starchy liquid. Heat the oil in a 20cm-diameter non-stick ovenproof frying pan over a medium heat. Season and press the grated potato into the pan so that it coats the base. Dot little lumps of butter over the top and cook in the oven for about 20 minutes.

Meanwhile, to make the pea mash, melt the butter in a saucepan over a medium heat until it is foaming. Add the peas and cook for about 4 minutes. Remove the pan from the heat and add the oil and mint leaves and then mash with a potato masher until the peas are roughly smooth. Season with sea salt and ground black pepper to taste and keep warm. For the goujons, fill a high-sided frying pan with 2.5–5cm of oil and place it over a high heat. It needs to be very hot when you start to fry. Coat the fish in the 3–4 tablespoons of flour, shake off the excess and set aside.

Place the 75g flour in a large mixing bowl, make a well in the middle, pour in a little beer and mix through. Add the beer and mix until you have a smooth batter. Season with ground black pepper and then drop a little of the batter into the hot oil; if it floats and puffs up, it's hot enough.

Working beside the pan, dip the fish goujons in the batter one at a time and then into the hot oil. Make sure not to overcrowd the pan as this will reduce the heat. Cook them for about 4 minutes until golden brown, turning halfway through the cooking time. Remove the goujons using a slotted spoon and place on a plate lined with kitchen paper.

Season generously with sea salt and ground black pepper. Serve with lemon wedges and a good helping of mushy mint peas and a quarter of the rosti.

Fish is often forgotten as the ultimate fast food. It is an incredibly quick cooking ingredient and I would normally wax lyrically about just how healthy it is too, but not in this recipe. No, this recipe is all about the nutty golden brown butter that forms the sauce alongside the tang of lemon juice and the salty hit from the capers. It's a bit of an all-in recipe and if you're going to make it, serve it with some steamed veggies for a delicious dinner.

SOLE MEUNIÈRE

SERVES 4

4 sole or plaice fillets, skin on
5 tbsp plain flour
Sea salt and ground black pepper
2 tbsp olive oil
100g butter
Juice of 1 lemon
3 tbsp capers, drained and rinsed
A little flat-leaf parsley,
    finely chopped, to garnish
    (optional)

Remove any prominent bones from the fish fillets using tweezers. Season the flour with salt and pepper on a large plate and press the fillets into the mix to coat on either side. Shake off any excess and set aside on a clean plate.

Heat the oil in a frying pan, which is big enough to accommodate the fish fillets over a high heat. Add the fish fillets, skin-side down, and cook for 2 minutes and then turn over and cook for a further minute until golden. Using a fish slice, remove the fillets from the pan and set aside on a warmed plate.

Place the pan back over a high heat and melt the butter until it is foaming, then add the lemon juice and capers and continue to cook until the butter turns a nutty golden brown. Pour the butter, lemon and caper mix over the fish and serve straight away garnished with the parsley, if using.

If you ever needed proof that something incredibly delicious can be made in a very short amount of time, then this salad is just that! Packed with punchy heat from the chorizo and salty squidginess from the halloumi, this little dish is full of wonderful things to keep you interested, even if you have very little time to make dinner. Speed up this recipe by buying sunblushed tomatoes intstead of roasting them yourself.

FLAVOUR BOMB SALAD

SERVES 4

300g cherry tomatoes, sliced in half

1 tbsp olive oil

1 tbsp balsamic vinegar

100g chorizo sausage, cut into chunky discs

200g halloumi cheese, cut into 1cm thick slices

Juice of ½ lemon

1 tbsp cider vinegar

1 garlic clove, peeled and finely chopped

Sea salt and ground black pepper

1 Baby Gem lettuce, leaves separated

200g chickpeas, drained and rinsed

½ red onion, peeled and finely sliced

Preheat the oven to 200°C (400°F), Gas Mark 6. Toss the tomatoes in a little olive oil and balsamic vinegar and place in a roasting tin. Roast in the oven for about 35 minutes until they have shrunk and become caramelised.

Meanwhile, dry fry the chorizo in a frying pan over a high heat until the discs are sizzling and coloured. Remove them from the pan using a slotted spoon and place on a plate lined with kitchen paper. Save the oil the chorizo has produced in the pan.

Place the frying pan back over the heat. Add a drop of olive oil if required and then fry the halloumi slices on both sides until they have a nice golden colour.

To make a dressing for the salad, pour the lemon juice into a bowl, then add the cider vinegar and garlic, season with sea salt and ground black pepper and whisk to combine.

In a large bowl, toss together the Baby Gem lettuce leaves with the dressing, chickpeas, chorizo and red onion and transfer to serving plates. Top with the halloumi slices and roasted cherry tomatoes and serve straight away.

What I love most about this recipe is that a big steaming pan of food is served straight to the table and people just dig in. It also makes a great leftover lunchbox if you're lucky enough to have any left.

SPICY SEAFOOD PAELLA

SERVES 4–6

12 prawns, shell on

2 garlic cloves, peeled and finely chopped

Good pinch of paprika, plus 1 tsp

A good grinding of black pepper

3 tbsp olive oil

150g chorizo sausage, cut into chunky discs

1 large onion, peeled and finely chopped

200g Arborio or paella rice

A few thyme sprigs

1 tsp turmeric

1 tsp cayenne pepper

125ml white wine

1 x 400g tin of cherry tomatoes

400ml fish stock

1 large squid, cut into rings

150g frozen peas

Good handful of flat-leaf parsley, finely chopped, to garnish

Lemon wedges, to serve

Put the prawns in a bowl and then add the garlic, paprika, black pepper and olive oil. Stir to coat the prawns and then set aside to marinate.

Meanwhile, dry fry the chorizo in a frying pan over a high heat until the discs are sizzling and coloured. Remove them from the pan using a slotted spoon and place on a plate lined with kitchen paper. Save the oil the chorizo has produced in the pan.

Cook the onion in the chorizo oil for about 6 minutes until softened, then add the rice, thyme, turmeric, cayenne and the remaining 1 teaspoon of paprika. Cook for 3 minutes, then pour in the wine and cook for 1 minute before adding the tomatoes and stock. Simmer for about 15 minutes, without stirring, then add the prawns (with the marinade) together with the squid, peas and chorizo. Simmer for 5 minutes.

Before serving, sprinkle over the parsley and tuck lemon wedges in around the sides. Serve straight to the table.

As sweet as it might sound, this dish is not named after the old lady who used to serve me lunch at school. It's a classic Italian recipe from Sicily supposedly named after the opera La Norma by Vincenzo Bellini. Like most pasta dishes, it's wonderfully simple to prepare and makes for a tasty weeknight supper. Use any pasta you like and try to get ricotta salata, a creamy cheese that makes a world of difference to the dish. If you can't find ricotta salata, you could use mozzarella.

PASTA ALLA NORMA

SERVES 4

1 large aubergine, cut into 3cm cubes
6 tbsp olive oil
Sea salt and ground black pepper
1 onion, peeled and finely chopped
1 tsp dried chilli flakes
6 garlic cloves, peeled and finely chopped
2 x 400g tins of plum tomatoes
Good handful of basil leaves
400g linguine
75g ricotta salata cheese, finely grated

Preheat the oven to 200°C (400°F), Gas Mark 6. Toss the aubergine in a mixing bowl with 4 tablespoons of olive oil and season with sea salt and ground black pepper. Transfer to a roasting tin and place in the oven to cook for 25 minutes.

While the aubergine is cooking, prepare the sauce. Heat the remaining 2 tablespoons of olive oil in a large saucepan over a medium heat. Add the onion and fry gently for 10 minutes, stirring occasionally, until softened. Add the chilli flakes and garlic and cook for a further 2 minutes. Pour in the tomatoes and use the back of a fork to mash them down. Mix through half the basil and season with sea salt and ground black pepper. Allow to simmer for 6 minutes.

Cook the pasta in a large pot of boiling salted water following the packet's instructions until al dente. Drain the pasta leaving a little water behind and place back into the pot along with the sauce and cooked aubergine. Mix through using a tongs. Serve straight away in warmed bowls garnished with the remaining basil and the ricotta salata.

FAST & HEALTHY

Turkey Noodle Lettuce Cups with Ginger Dipping Sauce 32/ Pad Thai 34/ Asian Shiitake Mushroom & Chicken Steam-Baked Bags 36/ Tomato Basil Tray Roast Fish Fillets with Gremolata 37/ Harissa Fish with Carrot & Mint Salad 38/ Za'Atar Pork Fillet with Jewelled Herby Pomegranate Couscous 40/ Lime & Coconut Chicken 42/ Margarita Chicken with Smoky Avocado Corn Salsa 44/ Griddled Beef & Mint Salad with Toasted Rice & Peanuts 46/ Blackened Salmon with Green Goddess Avocado Salad 48/ Butterflied Rosemary Chicken with Romesco Sauce & Simple Steamed Greens 50

I love the wonderful pure tastes and textures in this recipe. It's a light and healthy supper that can be made in a matter of minutes.

TURKEY NOODLE LETTUCE CUPS WITH GINGER DIPPING SAUCE

———

MAKES 15 CUPS

100g rice vermicelli noodles

1 tbsp sunflower oil

500g turkey mince

3 garlic cloves, peeled and finely
    chopped

1 thumb-sized piece of fresh ginger,
    peeled and finely grated

2 tbsp dark soy sauce

2 tbsp mirin

2 tbsp honey

Good handful of mint leaves,
    finely chopped

Good handful of coriander leaves,
    finely chopped

1 head of iceberg lettuce, leaves
    separated

75g roasted cashew nuts, roughly
    chopped

FOR THE DIPPING SAUCE

1 tbsp light soy sauce

1 tbsp mirin

2 tsp sesame oil

1 small thumb-sized piece of fresh
    ginger, peeled and finely grated

Soak the noodles in warm water until they are tender, then drain and set aside.

Mix the ingredients for the dipping sauce together in a bowl.

Heat the oil in a wok or a large high-sided frying pan over a high heat. Stir-fry the mince, breaking it up while you work, for about 3 minutes until it begins to get colour. Add the garlic and ginger and fry for 1 minute. Then stir in the soy sauce, mirin and honey. Turn off the heat and mix through the mint and coriander, saving a little aside for garnish.

Arrange the lettuce leaves on a serving platter and add a little portion of the noodles to each cup. Divide the cooked turkey on top and then sprinkle with the nuts and remaining coriander and mint. Roll up the lettuce leaves and dunk in the dipping sauce.

Rice noodles are a fantastic storecupboard ingredient and I regularly stock up at Asian markets where you can also buy jumbo-sized bottles of Asian staples like fish sauce, soy sauce, and so much more. This dish is possibly one of the most famous Thai dishes and appears on menus throughout the world. Rightfully so, it's a speedy dish full of deep layers of sweet and aromatic flavours.

PAD THAI

SERVES 4

250g flat rice noodles

3 garlic cloves, peeled and roughly chopped

Good handful of coriander leaves and stalks

1 red chilli, deseeded and roughly chopped

Grated zest and juice of 2 limes

2 tbsp sunflower oil

20 raw tiger prawns, de-shelled, heads and black vein removed

6 spring onions, trimmed and finely sliced

100g bean sprouts

3 tbsp Thai fish sauce (Nam Pla)

1 tbsp light soft brown sugar

2 large eggs, beaten

Lime wedges, to garnish

Good handful of salted peanuts, roughly chopped, to garnish

Soak the noodles in warm water until soft, then drain them and set aside. In a pestle and mortar, make a paste from the garlic, coriander stalks, red chilli and lime zest.

Heat the oil in a wok or a large non-stick frying pan over a high heat. When the oil is just at smoking point, add the paste and fry for about 1 minute until it becomes aromatic. Then add the prawns, half of the spring onions and bean sprouts and stir-fry for 2 minutes.

Add the drained noodles and mix through and then stir in the lime juice, fish sauce and brown sugar and cook for 2 minutes. Pour in the beaten eggs and mix through the noodles until just cooked.

Tumble the noodles out onto warmed serving plates and serve garnished with the coriander leaves, lime wedges, peanuts, and the remaining spring onions and bean sprouts.

There is something wonderfully wholesome about this rather special chicken supper. Served with a little steamed rice, this dinner will have you in tune with your inner zen in little or no time. Shiitake mushrooms are packed with all sorts of wonderful things and have been used in Chinese medicine for centuries – all the more reason to include them here.

ASIAN SHIITAKE MUSHROOM & CHICKEN STEAM-BAKED BAGS

SERVES 4

1 large thumb-sized piece of fresh ginger, peeled and finely grated

2 garlic cloves, peeled and finely grated

2 tbsp light soy sauce

2 tbsp mirin

2 tsp sesame oil

4 chicken breasts, sliced in half lengthways horizontally

4 large bok choy, sliced in half

150g shiitake mushrooms, sliced

½ Chinese cabbage, roughly sliced

100g sugar snap peas

6 spring onions, trimmed and finely sliced

Good handful of coriander leaves, to garnish

6 tbsp sesame seeds, toasted, to garnish

Preheat the oven to 200°C (400°F), Gas Mark 6. Line a large roasting tin with baking parchment.

In a bowl, mix together the ginger, garlic, soy sauce, mirin and sesame oil. Add the chicken and allow it to sit in the marinade while you prepare the rest of the dish.

Layer the prepared roasting tin with the bok choy, shiitake mushrooms, Chinese cabbage and sugar snap peas, making sure you leave space on each edge of the baking parchment for sealing. Place the chicken breast halves on top of the vegetables and then pour over the remaining marinade. Scatter over the spring onions.

Place another layer of baking parchment over the top. Fold all four sides in and seal with metal paper clips. Cook the whole tray in the oven on the middle shelf for 15–20 minutes until the chicken is cooked through. Serve the tray to the table garnished with a scattering of fresh coriander and some toasted sesame seeds.

Salty slices of prosciutto may not sound like the first companion of choice for meaty white fish fillets, but they add a salty bite and encourage the sweetness of the fish. I love the simplicity of a dish like this, which cooks quickly in the oven for 15 minutes and then is perked up at the end by a zingy gremolata of lemon zest, garlic and parsley.

TOMATO BASIL TRAY ROAST FISH FILLETS WITH GREMOLATA

SERVES 4

300g cherry tomatoes on the vine

Good handful of basil leaves

4 tbsp olive oil

2 tbsp balsamic vinegar

Sea salt and ground black pepper

4 large white fish fillets, such as whiting or haddock

150g thinly sliced prosciutto

1 lemon, zest grated and the fruit cut in half

2 garlic cloves, peeled and finely chopped

Good handful of flat-leaf parsley, finely chopped

Preheat the oven to 200°C (400°F), Gas Mark 6. Place the tomatoes in a large roasting tin together with most of the basil leaves. Drizzle over a little olive oil and balsamic vinegar and season with sea salt and ground black pepper. Toss together so the tomatoes are coated.

Wrap the fish fillets loosely with slices of prosciutto. Drizzle with a little olive oil and season with sea salt and ground black pepper, then lay the fillets among the tomatoes and pop in the oven for 15 minutes.

Meanwhile, prepare the gremolata by combining the lemon zest, garlic and parsley in a bowl and set aside.

When the fish is cooked, squeeze lemon juice over the roasting tin and then sprinkle each fillet with the gremolata and add a few fresh basil leaves. Serve straight away.

Proper healthy fast food for me must be packed with flavour and texture. Some rather healthy ingredients can easily be pumped up with the addition of heat and spice. Harissa is a north African spicy paste that can be made at home easily enough, but for a speedy supper, a jar from the local shops does nicely. The salad is incredibly simple to prepare, just grate the carrot and mix the dressing.

HARISSA FISH WITH CARROT & MINT SALAD

SERVES 2

2 tbsp harissa paste
2 small haddock fillets, skin removed
½ lemon
Sea salt and ground black pepper,
    to serve

FOR THE SALAD

1 tsp harissa paste
2 tbsp extra virgin olive oil
1 tsp balsamic vinegar
2 carrots, peeled and grated
2 spring onions, trimmed and
    finely sliced
Small handful of mint leaves,
    finely chopped

To prepare the fish, spread the harissa paste on the flesh side of the fish fillets and set aside.

For the salad, whisk together the harissa paste, olive oil and balsamic vinegar in a salad bowl and then toss in the carrots, spring onions and mint until combined.

Place a non-stick frying pan over a high heat and drizzle with a little oil if needed. Add the fish fillets, skin-side down, and fry for 2 minutes, then turn over and fry for a further 2 minutes or until cooked through. When you turn the fish, squeeze lemon juice over the top. Season the fish fillets and serve alongside the carrot salad and tuck in!

Za'atar is my latest discovery in the kitchen and I just can't get enough of it. It's a blend of fresh yet earthy Middle Eastern spices that can be sprinkled over meat and fish and is wonderful scattered over flatbreads drizzled with a little oil. For the couscous you can use any type you like, but if you can get your hands on Israeli couscous it's much bigger and has a meatier bite than the regular smaller grain.

ZA'ATAR PORK FILLET WITH JEWELLED HERBY POMEGRANATE COUSCOUS

SERVES 4

2 pork fillets
2 tbsp olive oil
5 tbsp natural yoghurt, to serve

FOR THE COUSCOUS

250g Israeli couscous
1 tbsp extra virgin olive oil
2 large handfuls of mint, coriander, flat-leaf parsley and oregano leaves, roughly chopped
1 x 400g tin of chickpeas, drained and rinsed
Seeds and juice of 1 pomegranate
1 lemon, zest grated and the fruit cut in half
Sea salt and ground black pepper

FOR THE ZA'ATAR

2 tbsp sesame seeds
4 tsp cumin seeds
4 tsp ground sumac
1 tsp sea salt
Good handful of oregano leaves, chopped

Soak the couscous in twice its volume of boiling water and cover with a plate. It's ready when it has soaked up all the water.

For the za'atar, toast the sesame and cumin seeds in a dry pan with an ovenproof handle placed over a medium-high heat for about 2 minutes until they are golden. Place the toasted seeds in a pestle and mortar with the sumac, salt and oregano and bash until you have a fine, fragrant and slightly moist powder.

Preheat the oven to 180°C (350°F), Gas Mark 4. Sprinkle the pork fillets with half the za'atar powder and press it into the flesh.

Place the frying pan back over a high heat and add a little oil. Sear the meat for a few minutes until it turns golden brown on all sides. Add a few tablespoons of water and place the pan in the oven to cook for 15 minutes until the pork is cooked through.

While the meat is in the oven, fluff up the couscous with a fork and stir in the oil, herbs, chickpeas, pomegranate juice and seeds and the lemon juice and zest. Squeeze over plenty of lemon juice and season with salt and ground black pepper to taste.

Remove the pork from the oven and slice in 1cm thick rounds. Serve on top of the couscous with a generous sprinkling of the remaining za'atar powder.

There is something altogether soothing about this recipe. The usual heat you'd expect from an Asian-inspired recipe bows out to make way for the more aromatic and fragrant coriander, lime zest and lemongrass, which is wrapped together by a creamy coconut broth. You could replace the chicken with prawns or sturdy vegetables like sweet potato.

LIME & COCONUT CHICKEN

SERVES 4

2 limes, zest grated and the fruit cut in half

Good handful of coriander leaves and stalks, roughly chopped

2 lemongrass stalks, roughly chopped

1 tbsp sunflower oil

1 x 400ml tin of light coconut milk

2 large chicken breasts, finely sliced

3 tbsp Thai fish sauce (Nam Pla)

1 tbsp light soy sauce

1 tsp sesame oil

Rice, to serve

Lime wedges, to serve

Good handful of coriander leaves, torn, to serve

1 red chilli, deseeded and finely sliced, to serve

1 spring onion, finely sliced, to serve

Blitz the lime zest, coriander stalks and lemongrass in a small hand blender until you have a smooth paste.

Heat the sunflower oil in a large wok over a high heat. Add the paste and fry for 1–2 minutes until it is aromatic. Add the coconut milk and mix through, then stir in the chicken strips and allow to cook on a gentle simmer for 10 minutes. Add the fish and soy sauces and simmer for a further 5 minutes. Squeeze over plenty of lime juice and mix through with the sesame oil.

Serve with rice, lime wedges and scatter over the coriander leaves, chilli and spring onions.

This recipe is all about big bold flavours and is one of my absolute favourite summer dishes. It's perfect for the BBQ, but if the weather doesn't hold up, a griddle pan will do just fine. This is lovely on a plate, but if you wanted, you could toast up some tortilla wraps in the pan and then serve slices of the chicken with the salsa and a generous dollop of sour cream.

MARGARITA CHICKEN WITH SMOKY AVOCADO CORN SALSA

SERVES 4

4 chicken breasts

3 garlic cloves, peeled and finely chopped

1 tsp ground cumin

1 tsp dried chilli flakes

1 tbsp dried oregano

1 lime, zest grated and the fruit cut in half

Sea salt and ground black pepper

1 tbsp sunflower oil

3 tbsp tequila

FOR THE SMOKY AVOCADO CORN SALSA

2 large corn on the cob

1 tbsp extra virgin olive oil, plus extra for brushing

2 large avocados, stoned and quartered

1 tbsp red wine vinegar

1 tsp smoky Tabasco sauce

1 garlic clove, peeled and finely chopped

1 small red onion, peeled and finely chopped

Good handful of coriander leaves

Lime wedges, to serve

Place the chicken on a sheet of baking parchment and spread each one with the garlic. Sprinkle over the cumin, chilli flakes, dried oregano and lime zest and season with sea salt and ground black pepper. Cover with another sheet of baking parchment and, using a rolling pin, bash the breasts until they are about 2cm thick.

Place the breasts on a plate and pour over the sunflower oil, tequila and a good squeeze of lime juice. Turn to coat and then allow to marinate while you prepare the salsa. If you have time, place the breasts in a resealable bag with the sunflower oil, tequila and lime juice and leave them to sit for an hour in the fridge.

Prepare the salsa by boiling the corn in a pan of water for 8–10 minutes until tender. Heat a large griddle pan over a high heat, brush the corn cobs with a little olive oil and place them on the griddle, turning when well charred. Then griddle the avocado quarters until you get nice char marks.

While the corn and avocado cook, combine the olive oil, vinegar, Tabasco sauce, garlic and red onion in a bowl. Using a knife, slice the cooked corn kernels off the cobs and then toss in the bowl with the onion and dressing. Add the coriander and season with sea salt and ground black pepper.

Brush the griddle pan with a little olive oil and add the chicken breasts along with the marinade. Cook for about 4 minutes on either side until the chicken is cooked through. Serve with a generous helping of the avocado and corn salsa and some lime wedges.

On my first visit to Bangkok, it was a hot and sticky night when we arrived and this was the dish we tucked into after wandering the streets. The rather interesting addition, to what would otherwise be an ordinary beef dish, is the toasted ground rice, which adds both texture and a surprisingly smoky, nutty flavour. The original dish doesn't feature the extra leaves, but I think it makes a wonderful healthy salad.

GRIDDLED BEEF & MINT SALAD WITH TOASTED RICE AND PEANUTS

SERVES 4

75g Thai sticky rice or basmati rice

2 x 200g sirloin steaks, each 2.5cm thick

Olive oil

1 red chilli, deseeded and finely sliced

4 shallots, peeled and finely sliced lengthways

1 lemongrass stalk, very finely sliced

1 large cucumber, peeled into thin ribbons

2 baby bok choy, finely sliced

100g sugar snap peas, finely sliced

Large handful of mint leaves

75g salted peanuts, roughly chopped

FOR THE DRESSING

1 tsp caster sugar

Grated zest and juice of 1 lime

3 tbsp Thai fish sauce (Nam Pla)

Place the dry rice in a pan over a medium-high heat and cook until it is toasted and a light golden brown colour. Place the hot rice into a pestle and mortar and bash until you have a rough powder.

In a large mixing bowl, prepare the dressing by whisking together the sugar and lime juice until the sugar has dissolved. Add the fish sauce, whisk through and set aside.

Place a large griddle pan over a high heat and massage the steaks with a little oil. Cook the steaks for 3–4 minutes on either side for medium rare. Remove from the pan and place on a plate under foil to rest for 5 minutes.

Add the chilli, shallots, lemongrass, cucumber, bok choy, sugar snap peas and half the mint leaves to the dressing and mix through.

Slice the steaks thinly and add it to the bowl with half the toasted rice and half the peanuts along with any of the remaining meat juices. Mix through and turn out onto a large serving dish. Garnish with the remaining toasted rice, peanuts and mint leaves.

Salmon is like the godfather of fish. Its big meaty fillets can stand up to just about any flavour you throw at it. Its oily flesh can withstand the heat of chilli and spice and, like most fish, it is incredibly healthy. The blackening method of this recipe creates a wonderful deep and smoky crust on the top of the fillets and, when combined with a cooling creamy avocado salad, it really is a delicious little dinner.

BLACKENED SALMON WITH GREEN GODDESS AVOCADO SALAD

SERVES 4

1 tsp paprika

1 tsp chilli powder

1 tsp cayenne pepper

1 tsp garlic powder

4 salmon fillets, skin on

3 tbsp olive oil or melted butter

FOR THE AVOCADO SALAD

1 head of romaine lettuce, leaves
  separated

6 radishes, trimmed and thinly sliced

2 large avocados, stoned and sliced

6 spring onions, trimmed and
  finely sliced

FOR THE DRESSING

3 tbsp buttermilk

1 tbsp olive oil

1 tbsp white wine vinegar

1 garlic clove, peeled and finely chopped

Handful of chives, snipped

Sea salt and ground black pepper

Preheat the grill to high. Mix the paprika, chilli powder, cayenne pepper and garlic powder on a flat plate. Drizzle the salmon fillets with olive oil or melted butter and then dip the tops in the spice mix.

Place on a grill tray and cook under the grill for about 10 minutes until the top is slightly charred and the fish is cooked all the way through.

While the fish is cooking, blitz the ingredients for the dressing in a hand blender until smooth. Season with sea salt and ground black pepper to taste.

On a large serving platter, arrange the romaine lettuce, radishes, avocados and spring onions and drizzle over the dressing. Place the salmon fillets on top and serve straight to the table.

Romesco is a fantastic Spanish pepper and nut sauce or salsa, which is a wonderful addition to grilled meat or fish. There are many variations, but essentially you are looking for a sweet, spiky, smoky relish. It's a super accompaniment to my butterflied chicken breasts and steamed greens.

BUTTERFLIED ROSEMARY CHICKEN WITH ROMESCO SAUCE & SIMPLE STEAMED GREENS

SERVES 4

4 chicken breasts

2 tbsp olive oil

3 garlic cloves, peeled and finely chopped

Grated zest of 1 lemon

2 rosemary sprigs, leaves picked and finely chopped

Sea salt and ground black pepper

150g tender stem broccoli

150g mangetout

FOR THE ROMESCO SAUCE

50g blanched almonds, toasted

50g skinless hazelnuts, toasted

6 garlic cloves, peeled and roughly chopped

6 tbsp extra virgin olive oil

2 tbsp red wine vinegar

1 tsp smoked paprika

1 slice of stale white bread, torn up (crusts are perfect)

½ red onion, peeled and roughly chopped

1 large tomato, peeled, deseeded and chopped

90g roasted red peppers from a jar

Good handful of flat-leaf parsley, finely chopped

Place the chicken breasts on a clean chopping board and, using a sharp knife, slice horizontally across each breast, but not the whole way across so the breasts can be opened like a book.

Whisk the olive oil, garlic, lemon zest and chopped rosemary together with some sea salt and ground black pepper in a bowl. Add the breasts and baste with the marinade. Leave to sit while you prepare the rest of the dish.

Cook the broccoli in a steamer over a little water for 3–4 minutes until tender, then add the mangetout and steam for another minute.

Prepare the romesco sauce by placing all the ingredients in a food processor and blitzing until they are combined but still have texture. Season with sea salt and ground black pepper.

Place a large non-stick frying pan over a medium-high heat. Add the chicken and fry for 2–3 minutes on either side until cooked all the way through. Serve the chicken with the romesco sauce and the steamed vegetables.

PROPER COMFORT FOOD

Boeuf Bourginon 54/ Roast Asian Beef Stew with Chilli Noodles 56/ Eight Degrees Braised Shoulder of Lamb with Butter Bean Mash 58/ Deep, Dark & Delicious Pork Shoulder Tacos 60/ Rich Tomato Shellfish Soup 61/ Baked Risotto all'Arrabiata 62/ Toulouse Sausage Puy Lentil Stew 64/ Three-Cheese Lasagne 66/ One-pot Whole Chicken with White Wine Root Veg & Shallots 68/ Roast Chicken Cacciatore 70/ Chorizo Chicken Bean Stew 72/ Howth Head Seafood Chowder 74/ Honey & Orange Roast Carrot Bulgur Salad 76

Thanks to the film *Julie & Julia* now every time the classic French dish boeuf bourginon is mentioned all I can think of is Julia Child. Although this dish was a regular in mom's repertoire, I have had to consult *Mastering the Art of French Cooking* to make sure this comfort food classic would get the approval of Mrs Child. It's a rich and deeply flavoured dish, which sings comfort and is ideal for cold winter weekends.

BOEUF BOURGINON

SERVES 4

900g chuck steak cut into 3cm cubes

2 tbsp olive oil

150g streaky bacon, sliced

1 large carrot, peeled and sliced

1 large onion, peeled and sliced

3 garlic cloves, peeled and finely chopped

2 tbsp plain flour

500ml red wine

300ml beef stock

1 bay leaf

1 tbsp tomato purée

Sea salt and ground black pepper

18 pearl onions or small shallots, peeled

300g button mushrooms, wiped and
  left whole

Good handful of flat-leaf parsley,
  roughly chopped, to serve

Preheat the oven to 150°C (300°F), Gas Mark 2. Place the steak pieces on a plate and pat dry with kitchen paper.

Heat 1 tablespoon of the oil in a heavy casserole pot with a lid over a medium-high heat. Add the steak pieces and brown on all sides so they have a deep brown colour. Don't overcrowd the pot or you won't get a good colour on the meat so it's best to do this in batches. With the last batch add in the bacon and fry until it is sizzling and golden.

Remove the steak pieces and bacon from the pot with a slotted spoon and place on a plate lined with kitchen paper. Add the carrot and onion and fry the vegetables for about 6 minutes until the onion has softened. Stir through the garlic, then return the steak pieces and bacon back to the pan and add the flour. Cook for 4 minutes, stirring every now and then.

Pour in the wine, beef stock and the bay leaf, add the tomato purée and stir through. Season with sea salt and ground black pepper and bring to a steady simmer. Cover the pot and place it in the oven to cook very slowly for 3 hours until the liquid has reduced by half and the meat is incredibly tender when pierced with a fork.

About 20 minutes before serving, fry the pearl onions and mushrooms in a non-stick frying pan over a medium-high heat with the remaining oil for about 6 minutes until they are tender. Add these to the casserole 10 minutes before the end of the cooking time. Serve with creamy mashed potato and freshly chopped parsley scattered over the top.

Harnessing aromatic Asian ingredients creates a wonderfully alternative dark and delicious beef stew. Serve it with the noodles suggested here or with some plain steamed rice for an altogether different comforting supper.

ROAST ASIAN BEEF STEW WITH CHILLI NOODLES

SERVES 6–8

1 tbsp szechuan peppercorns

6 whole star anise

100ml dark soy sauce

2 tbsp sesame oil

3 garlic cloves, peeled and finely chopped

1 thumb-sized piece of fresh ginger, peeled and finely chopped

1.5kg beef topside or rump steak, cut into 3cm cubes

2 tsp Chinese five-spice powder

3 tbsp sunflower oil

3 tbsp plain flour

2 onions, peeled, halved and sliced in half moons

2 carrots, peeled and roughly diced

1 litre beef stock

300g egg noodles

1 red pepper, deseeded and cut into slices

1 green pepper, deseeded and cut into slices

2 red chillies, deseeded and finely chopped

8 spring onions, trimmed and finely sliced on the diagonal

1 tbsp chilli oil

Good handful of coriander leaves

Toast the szechuan peppercorns and star anise in a dry frying pan over a medium heat until they become aromatic. Remove to a plate and allow to cool.

In a large bowl, mix the soy sauce, sesame oil, garlic and ginger. Add the meat and five-spice powder, peppercorns and star anise and toss until the meat is evenly coated. Cover and leave in the fridge to marinate for 2 hours or overnight.

When you are ready to cook the stew, preheat the oven to 160°C (325°F), Gas Mark 3. Heat a little of the sunflower oil in a large casserole with a lid over a medium-high heat. Add the meat and its marinade and fry for about 4 minutes until the meat has a little colour. Add the flour, onions and carrots and continue to cook for about 4 minutes until the onions have softened.

Pour in the beef stock and bring the stew to a steady simmer. Cover with the lid and cook in the oven for about 1½ hours until the meat is tender.

Cook the noodles in a large pot of boiling water according to the packet's instructions until they are tender. Drain the noodles and set aside.

Heat some more of the sunflower oil in a large wok over a medium heat. Add the peppers, chillies and half the spring onions and fry for about 5 minutes until the peppers are tender. Add the noodles and the chilli oil and fry until they are heated through.

Serve generous portions of noodles with the beef stew on top and a sprinkling of coriander leaves and the remaining spring onions.

Slow-cooked until tender and falling of the bone, the cheaper cuts of meat are key ingredients to some of the best comfort food dishes. My fellow food blogger friend Caroline Hennessy and her partner run the Eight Degrees Brewing company in Cork producing a selection of artisan beers and ales. Their sunburnt Irish red ale is the perfect cooking liquor for this braised lamb shoulder.

EIGHT DEGREES BRAISED SHOULDER OF LAMB WITH BUTTER BEAN MASH

SERVES 6

3 garlic cloves, peeled and roughly chopped

3 thyme sprigs, leaves picked and roughly chopped

3 rosemary sprigs, leaves picked and roughly chopped

Sea salt and ground black pepper

1–2 tbsp olive oil

2kg lamb shoulder, boned and rolled

2 onions, peeled and roughly chopped

2 celery stalks, trimmed and roughly chopped

3 large carrots, peeled and roughly chopped

250ml red ale or dark beer

250ml lamb or beef stock

1 bay leaf

FOR THE BUTTER BEAN MASH

1 tbsp plain flour

Sea salt and ground black pepper

3 tbsp olive oil

3 garlic cloves, peeled and finely sliced

Grated zest and juice of 1 lemon

1 rosemary sprig

2 x 400g tins of butter beans, drained and rinsed

Small handful flat-leaf parsley, chopped, to serve

Preheat the oven to 150°C (300°F), Gas Mark 2. In a pestle and mortar, bash together the garlic, thyme, rosemary and some sea salt until you have a coarse paste.

Heat a little of the oil in a large casserole with a lid over a high heat. Add the lamb and brown it on all sides until it has a golden brown colour. Remove the lamb from the casserole with a slotted spoon and set aside on a plate and allow to cool. Add a little extra oil to the pot if required, add the onions, celery and carrots and cook for about 6 minutes until the onions have softened.

Meanwhile, using a small sharp knife, poke holes in the lamb and then rub all over with the garlic and herb paste, pushing it into the holes as you go. Pour in the ale and stock, add the lamb on top, pop in the bay leaf and bring to a steady simmer. Cover with the lid and place in the oven to cook for about 4 hours until the meat falls away from the bone. Baste with the liquid at regular intervals.

Remove the lamb from the pot and leave it to rest on a chopping board under foil while you prepare the butter bean mash. Spoon any fat from the top of the lamb cooking liquid and place the pot over a high heat. Whisk through the flour and simmer until it thickens slightly, stirring continuously. Season with sea salt and ground black pepper to taste.

Heat the olive oil in a large frying pan over a low heat. Add the garlic, lemon zest and juice and rosemary and fry very gently until the oil becomes aromatic. Remove the rosemary and add the beans. Using a potato masher, roughly mash the beans leaving a few whole.

Serve slices of the lamb with the butter bean mash and a generous amount of gravy. Scatter with some chopped parsley.

I am aware that tacos don't instantly scream comfort food, but this method of slow cooking the pork until it is tender and sticky ticks all the boxes in terms of the warmth and comfort I need.

DEEP, DARK & DELICIOUS PORK SHOULDER TACOS

SERVES 6-8

1.5kg boneless pork shoulder
20 small tortilla wraps
Garnishes of choice, such as finely
    sliced red onion, salsa, sour cream,
    coriander and lime wedges

FOR THE MARINADE

Large handful of coriander leaves
Grated zest and juice of 1 lime
1 large onion, peeled and finely
    chopped
8 garlic cloves, peeled and roughly
    chopped
1 tbsp Tabasco sauce
2 tsp ground coriander
2 tsp ground cumin
2 tsp dried oregano
100ml distilled white vinegar
500ml beer
3 tbsp treacle
Sea salt

Blitz all the ingredients for the marinade in a blender or pestle and mortar until you have a smooth mixture.

Place the pork in a large pot with a lid, spoon the marinade over the meat and turn the pork until it is coated all over. Cover and allow the meat to marinate in the spicy mix for a couple of hours or overnight if you have the time. If you don't have the time, don't worry just cook the meat.

When you are ready to cook the meat, place the pot over a high heat, add just enough water (about 500ml) to cover the meat and bring it to the boil. Reduce the heat, cover with a lid and cook at a steady simmer for about 1½ hours until the meat pulls apart easily with a fork. Make sure to turn the pork during cooking.

Remove the pork from the sauce with a carving fork and shred, then place the shredded meat on a warmed plate, cover with foil and set aside. Bring the sauce to a steady simmer and reduce until it is thick. Add the shredded meat back to the pan and heat through.

Warm the tortilla wraps in foil in the oven or in a frying pan. Serve the pot of sticky shredded pork meat straight to the table with garnishes of your choice and the tortilla wraps and get stuck in!

This soup makes a lovely spicy shellfish broth that is perfect for a cold winter's day. You can also add white fish cut into chunks to this soup at the same time as the mussels.

RICH TOMATO SHELLFISH SOUP

SERVES 6

150g chorizo sausage, cut into cubes

A drop of rapeseed oil (optional)

1 onion, peeled and finely chopped

1 fennel bulb, thinly sliced

2 celery stalks, trimmed and thinly sliced

2 x 400g tins of chopped tomatoes

3 tbsp tomato paste

1 bay leaf

3 garlic cloves, peeled and finely chopped

1 red chilli, deseeded and finely chopped

125ml white wine

1 litre fish stock

3 potatoes, peeled and cut into 2cm chunks

Sea salt and ground black pepper

12 mussels, cleaned

16 large raw prawns

Large handful of flat-leaf parsley, roughly chopped

Dry-fry the chorizo in a large pot over a medium heat until the cubes are crisp. Remove the chorizo from the pot with a slotted spoon, place on a plate and set aside.

You should be left with plenty of the fat and oils rendered from the chorizo while they cooked, but if not, add a drop of rapeseed oil. Add the onion, fennel and celery and sweat for about 10 minutes until the vegetables have softened.

Add the tomatoes, tomato paste, bay leaf, garlic, chilli and white wine and cook for about 15 minutes over a medium heat until the sauce has reduced slightly. Pour in the fish stock and stir in the potatoes. Simmer for about 15 minutes until the potatoes are just cooked and then season with sea salt and ground black pepper to taste. Add the mussels and cook for 3 minutes until they have opened, then add the prawns and cook for a further 2–3 minutes until all the seafood is cooked through. Discard any mussels which haven't opened during cooking.

Serve straight away in deep warmed bowls with a scattering of chopped parsley. Make sure you serve some crusty bread to mop up the juices.

A baked risotto takes away the need to stand by the stove stirring for 20 minutes. Instead it cooks gently in the oven until the rice is plump. This version has a spicy tomato taste to it but, as with all risottos, there are many different variations you could try, such as wild mushroom, roast squash or pea and asparagus.

BAKED RISOTTO ALL'ARRABIATA

SERVES 4

1 tbsp olive oil

8 rashers of pancetta or smoked streaky bacon, sliced

50g butter

1 onion, peeled and finely chopped

300g risotto rice, such as Arborio

1–2 tsp dried chilli flakes, to taste

75ml red wine

1 litre chicken stock

250ml tomato sauce or passata

Sea salt and ground black pepper

75g Parmesan cheese, grated

A few basil leaves, to serve

Preheat the oven to 180°C (350°F), Gas Mark 4. Heat the oil in a frying pan over a medium heat. Add the pancetta or bacon and fry it until it is crisp. Remove from the pan with a slotted spoon on to a plate lined with kitchen paper, reserving the fat in the pan.

Melt half of the butter in the pan, then add the onion and fry gently for 5–8 minutes until it has softened. Add the rice and chilli flakes and stir for 1 minute until coated. Pour in the red wine and let it bubble for 1 minute, then add the stock and tomato sauce and return the pancetta or bacon to the pan. Bring it to the boil and season with sea salt and ground black pepper to taste.

Transfer the risotto to a baking dish, cover it with foil and cook in the oven for about 20 minutes until the rice is plump and cooked through. Remove the dish from the oven and allow it to sit, covered, for 5 minutes. This will give the risotto time to finish cooking and absorb the rest of the liquid. Gently stir in the remaining butter together with the Parmesan cheese.

Add more salt and pepper, if necessary, then serve topped with basil leaves.

If you thought there was no way you could turn the humble sausage into a sophisticated dish, well frankly, you thought wrong. This sausage and lentil stew is elegant enough to serve at a dinner party, but is still warm and comforting enough to snaffle from a bowl in front of the TV. Do try to get your hands on some good-quality sausages for this dish and make sure to use Puy lentils as they hold their shape far better than other varieties.

TOULOUSE SAUSAGE PUY LENTIL STEW

SERVES 6

1 tbsp olive oil

6–8 large Toulouse or butcher's sausages

150g pancetta or smoked streaky bacon, cut into pieces

2 carrots, peeled and finely chopped

1 large onion, peeled and finely chopped

2 celery stalks, trimmed and finely chopped

1 tbsp tomato purée

1 tbsp Dijon mustard

75ml red wine

300g Puy lentils

A few thyme sprigs

500ml chicken stock

Sea salt and ground black pepper

Heat the oil in a large high-sided frying pan over a medium-high heat. Add the sausages and brown them on all sides. Remove the sausages from the pan and set aside, then add the pancetta or bacon with the carrots, onion and celery and fry until the bacon is sizzling. Stir through the tomato purée, Dijon mustard and red wine.

Add the lentils, thyme and stock, season with sea salt and ground black pepper and bring to the boil. Cook for 15 minutes then add the sausages, nuzzling them among the lentils.

Cook for a further 10 minutes or until the lentils are tender. Add a splash of water to the pan if it begins to look a little dry before the lentils are cooked. Carry the pot straight to the table and serve on warmed plates.

I cry a little bit inside when I see ready meal lasagnes cut in brick-like wedges, ready for the microwave. A really good lasagne is truly a thing of beauty and should be treated as such. They take time, effort and love and the end result should be layers of rich meat sauce, creamy white sauce and perfectly cooked pasta. There are many different variations on this classic and this one features a rich white sauce with three different cheeses, which adds a wonderful dimension to the dish.

THREE-CHEESE LASAGNE

SERVES 6

2 tbsp olive oil

500g beef mince

8 rashers of smoked streaky bacon, roughly chopped

1 onion, peeled and finely chopped

2 garlic cloves, peeled and finely chopped

1 small carrot, peeled and coarsely grated

75g mushrooms, finely chopped

2 x 400g tins of chopped tomatoes

1 tbsp tomato purée

250ml red wine

1 tsp dried oregano

Sea salt and ground black pepper

Handful of basil leaves, chopped

6–8 sheets of lasagne

FOR THE CHEESE SAUCE

50g butter

50g plain flour

300ml warm milk

75g blue cheese, crumbled

75g Cheddar cheese, grated

50g Parmesan cheese, grated

1 tsp English mustard

Heat 1 tablespoon of the olive oil in a large frying pan over a medium heat. Add the mince and fry for 2–3 minutes until browned. Remove the mince from the pan and set aside on a plate.

Heat the rest of the oil in the frying pan, then add the bacon and fry for about 2 minutes until cooked through. Add the onion and garlic and fry for a further 2 minutes, then stir in the carrot and mushrooms and fry for 2 minutes more. Return the mince to the pan with the tomatoes, tomato purée, red wine and oregano. Bring to the boil, then reduce the heat and simmer for 15–20 minutes. Season with sea salt and ground black pepper to taste, then stir through the basil.

Preheat the oven to 190°C (375°F), Gas mark 5.

To make the cheese sauce, melt the butter in a saucepan and stir in the flour quickly so you have a smooth paste. Gradually whisk in the warm milk and bring the sauce to the boil. Reduce the heat to a steady simmer and simmer for 2 minutes until the sauce becomes thick. Remove the pan from the heat and add the cheeses (saving a little of the blue cheese and Cheddar for sprinkling on the top) and English mustard. Season with sea salt and ground black pepper.

Spoon a layer of the Bolognese into a high-sided 27.5 x 20cm baking dish, then top with a layer of lasagne sheets followed by a layer of the cheese sauce. Repeat the process until the Bolognese and cheese sauces are used up, finishing with a layer of cheese sauce. Sprinkle the reserved cheese over the top and bake in the oven for 30–35 minutes until the lasagne is bubbling and browned on top. Serve straight to the table.

I have a special place in my heart for one-pot suppers. Perhaps it's the process of bundling everything into a big casserole and then leaving it to simmer away in the oven that really comforts me, or maybe it's the fact there isn't much to wash up afterwards. Either way this one-pot chicken recipe makes a wonderful winter family dinner.

ONE-POT WHOLE CHICKEN WITH WHITE WINE ROOT VEG & SHALLOTS

SERVES 4

1 whole chicken (approx. 1.2kg)
Sea salt and ground black pepper
1 lemon, halved
1 garlic bulb, halved horizontally
3 tbsp olive oil
3 carrots, peeled and roughly chopped
3 parsnips, peeled and roughly chopped
6 small shallots, peeled
500ml white wine
250ml chicken stock
6 thyme sprigs
Small handful of flat-leaf parsley, roughly chopped, to garnish

Preheat the oven 200°C (400°F), Gas Mark 6. Season the chicken all over with sea salt and ground black pepper. Stuff the cavity with the lemon halves and garlic bulb and tie the legs together with kitchen string.

Heat the oil in a large ovenproof casserole pot over a high heat. Add the chicken and brown it on all sides until you have a golden brown colour. Remove the chicken from the pot and set aside.

Add the carrots, parsnips and shallots and fry for about 5 minutes until just tender. Then pour in the white wine and allow to bubble for 3 minutes before adding the stock and thyme. Return the chicken to the pot and bring the liquid to the boil. Check the seasoning and then cover with the lid and pop in the oven to cook for 1¼ hours or until the chicken is cooked all the way through. Leave to rest for 10 minutes.

Remove the chicken from the pot and carve. Take the lemon and garlic out of the cavity and squeeze the juice from the lemon and the cloves from the bulb and add to the cooking liquid, whisking in to combine.

Serve portions of the chicken in deep bowls with the vegetables and cooking juices. Garnish with parsley.

Like every classic recipe that has become famous throughout the world, there are, of course, many variations. Cacciatore means 'hunter's style' and is a traditional Italian dish that consists of chicken or rabbit with tomatoes and onion. My version is a tray roast, which makes the sauce deep and sweet. I also add mascarpone to the sauce to make it creamy and put basil in the sauce for a sweet aniseed taste.

ROAST CHICKEN CACCIATORE

SERVES 6

1–2 tbsp olive oil

6 chicken breasts on the bone with skin on

1 large onion, peeled and finely sliced

2 garlic cloves, peeled and finely sliced

1 red pepper, deseeded and finely sliced

1 tsp dried oregano

150ml white wine

2 x 400g tins of plum tomatoes

Good handful of basil leaves, torn

Sea salt and ground black pepper

4 tbsp mascarpone cheese

Grated zest of 1 lemon

Preheat the oven to 200°C (400°F), Gas Mark 6.

Heat some of the oil in a large non-stick frying pan over a high heat. Add the chicken and brown it on all sides until it has a good colour. Remove from the pan and set aside on a plate.

Add a little more oil to the pan, if required, then fry the onion, garlic and pepper for 5–6 minutes until the onion has softened. Stir through the oregano, then pour in the wine and tomatoes and bring to a steady simmer. Stir through half the basil and season with sea salt and ground black pepper.

Pour half the sauce into a baking dish and place the browned chicken on top with any resting juices from the plate. Pour over the remaining sauce and roast in the oven for about 30 minutes until the chicken is cooked through and tender.

Remove the chicken from the oven and stir through the mascarpone cheese. Garnish with the remaining basil leaves and the lemon zest and serve straight to the table.

Chorizo adds a wonderful warmth and subtle heat to this great chicken stew. I use plum tomatoes here as they have a much better flavour than chopped tomatoes.

CHORIZO CHICKEN BEAN STEW

SERVES 6

1 tbsp olive oil

150g chorizo sausage, cut into chunky discs

6 chicken legs

Sea salt and ground black pepper

1 large red onion, peeled and finely chopped

3 garlic cloves, peeled and finely chopped

150ml red wine

2 x 400g tins of plum tomatoes

500ml chicken stock

1 x 400g tin of cannellini beans, drained and rinsed

Flat-leaf parsley, to garnish

Crusty bread, to serve

Heat the oil in a large casserole over a high heat. Add the chorizo and fry until it is sizzling and roaring red. Remove the chorizo from the pan with a slotted spoon leaving the red oils behind.

Season the chicken legs with sea salt and ground black pepper and add them to the pan in batches, browning until they have a good colour on all sides. Set aside with the chorizo.

Fry the onion and garlic for 5 minutes until the onion has softened. Pour in the red wine and tip in the tomatoes. Using a potato masher or the back of a fork, roughly mash the tomatoes, then pour in the stock and bring the liquid to a steady boil.

Return the chicken legs and chorizo to the stew. Bring back to the boil, cover with a lid and simmer for about 1 hour until the chicken is cooked all the way through.

About 5 minutes before you serve, stir through the beans and once they are warm, serve generous portions of the stew in deep warmed dishes. Garnish with flat-leaf parsley and dig in with lots of crusty bread on the table to mop up all those delicious juices.

My home town of Howth is famous throughout Ireland for its fish. Along the west pier there are plenty of fishmongers to choose some of the freshest fish for supper. This wonderfully creamy seafood chowder always reminds me of home and with a few slices of brown bread with Irish salted butter, I'm there in an instant.

HOWTH HEAD SEAFOOD CHOWDER

SERVES 6

1 tbsp unsalted butter

1 onion, peeled and finely chopped

50g pancetta, cut into cubes

2 thyme sprigs, leaves picked

1 bay leaf

300g potatoes, peeled and chopped

1 litre fish stock

Sea salt and ground black pepper

150g cod or haddock, skinned and flesh cut into 2cm pieces

150g salmon, skinned and flesh cut into 2cm pieces

250g undyed smoked haddock, skinned and flesh cut into 2cm pieces

1kg mussels in their shells, cleaned

1 tbsp finely chopped flat-leaf parsley

160ml double cream

Smoked salmon, cut into strips, to garnish

Melt the butter in a large pot over a medium-high heat. Add the onion and fry for 3–4 minutes until softened. Add the pancetta and continue to fry until it colours, then stir in the thyme leaves, bay leaf and potatoes and cook gently for 2–3 minutes before adding the fish stock. Season well with sea salt and ground black pepper.

Simmer for 10–15 minutes until the potatoes are tender yet firm. Add the cod, salmon, smoked haddock and mussels and simmer gently for 5 minutes. Discard any mussels which haven't opened whilst cooking.

Remove the pot from the heat and gently stir through the parsley and cream. Try not to stir too vigorously as the fish chunks will break up. Serve in warmed deep bowls with the strips of smoked salmon as a garnish on top.

The sweetness of warm roast carrots dressed with a honey and orange dressing allow for comfort and health in the darkest days of winter.

HONEY & ORANGE ROAST CARROT BULGUR SALAD

SERVES 4 (V)

600g small sweet carrots, sliced in half

1 tbsp olive oil

1 tbsp honey

4 thyme sprigs, leaves picked

1 tsp cumin seeds

Grated zest of 1 orange

Sea salt and ground black pepper

250g bulgur wheat

50g pine nuts, toasted

Good handful of salad leaves

2 large avocados, stoned and sliced

FOR THE DRESSING

3 tbsp extra virgin olive oil

Juice of ½ orange

1 tbsp balsamic vinegar

1 tbsp honey

1 heaped tsp wholegrain mustard

Preheat the oven to 180°C (350°F), Gas Mark 4. Place the carrots in a large roasting tin and drizzle with the olive oil and honey. Sprinkle over the thyme, cumin seeds and orange zest, then season with sea salt and ground black pepper and toss to coat. Cook in the oven for 40–50 minutes or until the carrots are tender when pierced with a fork.

While the carrots are in the oven, soak the bulgur wheat in twice its volume of boiling water until it is plumped up and tender. Toss through the toasted pine nuts. Whisk together the ingredients for the dressing in a large mixing bowl, then toss in the salad leaves and avocados.

When the carrots are cooked, assemble the salad by placing a generous amount of bulgur wheat on the plate. Top with the carrots and the dressed leaves and avocados. Spoon over any remaining dressing and eat up.

FOOD TO SHARE

Turkish Ground Meat Pizza 80/ Blue Cheese Beef Sliders 82/ Homemade Spring Rolls with Dipping Sauce 84/ Bun Cha: Barbecued Pork Skewers with Herbs & Rice Vermicelli 86/ Pork Pot Stickers with Warm Bok Choy & Cashews 88/ Buttermilk Fried Chicken with Sweet Potato Fries 90/ Jerk Chicken with Mango Salsa 92/ Spring Pea & Ricotta Ravioli 94/ Mexican Fish Tacos 96/ Mini Goat's Cheese, Spinach & Prosciutto Calzone 98/ Surf & Turf Salad 100/ Saturday Night Teriyaki Chicken 102

Lahmacun or Turkish pizza is a subtly spiced, meaty flat-bread that can easily be prepared at home. In Turkey it's fast food fare, but makes for wonderful party food to share.

TURKISH GROUND MEAT PIZZA

SERVES 6

FOR THE DOUGH

300ml full fat milk

7g sachet of easy blend dried yeast

1 tsp sugar

500g strong white flour, plus extra
  for dusting

1 tbsp nigella seeds

1 tsp salt

4 tbsp melted butter

FOR THE TOPPING

2 large eggs

350g lamb mince

2 large tomatoes, peeled, deseeded and
  finely chopped

Good handful of flat-leaf parsley,
  chopped

1 large red onion, peeled and finely
  chopped

3 garlic cloves, peeled and finely
  chopped

1 tsp dried chilli flakes

2 tsp cumin seeds

1 tsp coriander seeds

1 tbsp honey

Sea salt and ground black pepper

To make the dough, warm the milk and stir in the yeast and sugar until they have dissolved. Allow the mixture to sit for 5 minutes.

Combine the flour, nigella seeds and salt in a large bowl. Make a small well with your hands and pour the yeast, milk and sugar mixture into the well together with the butter. Combine the mix until you have a rough dough.

Turn the dough out onto a lightly floured surface and knead it for 6–8 minutes until it is smooth and elastic. Set the dough aside under a damp tea towel in a warm spot to rise for about 45 minutes or until it has doubled in size. Mix all the ingredients for the topping in a bowl, season with sea salt and ground black pepper and set aside.

Preheat the oven at 240°C (475°F), Gas Mark 9 and add the pizza stone if using. When the dough has risen, divide it into six egg-sized balls and flatten them into long oval shapes on a work surface dusted with semolina or a little flour.

Transfer the ovals to a pizza stone or baking sheet. Spread the meat mix on the flattened dough, making sure you leave about 2cm all around for the crust. Place in the oven to cook for 15 minutes until the edges are golden brown. Cut them into slices and serve straight away.

If you haven't heard of sliders before, they are an American invention and are basically mini burgers. They are perfect for party nibbles and this particular recipe has sweet caramelised onion and salty blue cheese served alongside.

BLUE CHEESE BEEF SLIDERS

SERVES 4

2 tbsp rapeseed oil

2 red onions, peeled and finely sliced

Sea salt and ground black pepper

500g beef mince

1 heaped tsp Dijon mustard

1 tbsp Worcestershire sauce

60g blue cheese, cut into 8 slices

8 mini burger baps

2 Baby Gem lettuce, leaves separated

2 large tomatoes, cut into slices, to garnish

8 cornichons, to garnish

Tomato ketchup, to serve

Heat 1 tablespoon of the oil in a frying pan over a high heat. Add the red onions and cook for a few minutes until they are slightly coloured, then reduce the heat and cook gently for about 8 minutes until softened right down. Season with sea salt and set aside to cool completely.

Combine the beef, mustard and Worcestershire sauce in a large mixing bowl and season with sea salt and ground black pepper. Form the meat mixture into 8 mini burger patties and place on a plate, cover with cling film and set aside in the fridge until you are ready to fry them.

To cook the burgers, heat the remaining oil in a large frying pan over a high heat. Fry the burgers for 3 minutes on either side until they are cooked all the way through. When you turn the burgers in the pan, add a slice of blue cheese to each one.

To serve, split the bread baps and fill with Baby Gem lettuce leaves, a slice of tomato, the burgers, some caramelised onions and a good dollop of ketchup – add some cornichons on the side!

When I was growing up, my favourite dishes to cook were Asian and these spring rolls were made to death in my house. They are very simple to prepare and always look impressive when produced for friends. Of course there are many variations and you could add chopped prawns, chicken mince or even sweet potato to the filling.

HOMEMADE SPRING ROLLS WITH DIPPING SAUCE

MAKES 12 SPRING ROLLS

About 1 tbsp olive oil

200g pork mince

1 thumb-sized piece of fresh ginger, peeled and finely chopped

4 spring onions, trimmed and roughly chopped

2 garlic cloves, peeled and finely chopped

150g carrots, peeled and grated

1 red pepper, deseeded and finely sliced

200g Chinese cabbage, thinly shredded

Small handful of coriander leaves and stalks, finely chopped

1 tbsp light soy sauce

1 tbsp rice wine

1 tsp caster sugar

1 tsp sesame oil

12 spring roll skins

Sunflower oil, for frying

FOR THE DIPPING SAUCE

1 tbsp grated ginger

2 tsp caster sugar

5 tbsp light soy sauce

1 tbsp rice wine

1 tsp sesame oil

1 bird's eye chilli, deseeded and finely sliced

Small handful of coriander sprigs, to garnish

Heat a drop of the olive oil in a large frying pan over a medium-high heat. Add the pork mince and cook it for about 5 minutes until browned all over, then remove it from the pan and set aside.

Add an extra drop of the oil to the pan and stir in the ginger, spring onions and garlic. Stir-fry for about 1 minute, then add the carrots, red pepper, Chinese cabbage and coriander stalks and fry for about 5 minutes until the carrot is tender.

Return the pork to the pan and add the soy sauce, rice wine and caster sugar and fry for a further 2 minutes. Stir through the sesame oil and then remove the pan from the heat and allow it to cool completely.

Whisk all the ingredients for the dipping sauce together and set aside.

Assemble the spring rolls one at a time, by placing one spring roll skin on a work surface and adding 2 tablespoons of the cooled mixture diagonally across the centre in a small sausage shape. Fold each side in and then roll up tightly.

Fill a large high-sided frying pan with 1–2cm of the sunflower oil and then place this over a high heat. Check that the oil is hot enough to fry the spring rolls by dipping one into the oil and seeing if it bubbles vigorously.

Shallow-fry the spring rolls, seam-side down, for 3–4 minutes on either side until they are an evenly golden colour all over. Remove from the oil with a slotted spoon and set aside on a plate lined with kitchen paper. Serve the spring rolls straight away with the dipping sauce and garnished with coriander sprigs.

Vietnam is all about incredible street food and when I visited the country, this was one of my favourite dishes to eat on a plastic stool at a roadside pop-up vendor. It's a feast of smoky pork skewers, wrapped in lettuce leaves with fresh herbs and dipped in a salty sweet sauce. Barbecue the pork to get the essential smoky element of South East Asian cooking, but a griddle pan will also work. The classic version uses pork belly to form little pork patties, but this is a quicker variation.

BUN CHA: BARBECUED PORK SKEWERS WITH HERBS & RICE VERMICELLI

SERVES 6

3 garlic cloves, peeled

Grated zest and juice of 1 lime

2 large handfuls of coriander leaves and stalks

8 spring onions, trimmed and finely sliced

1 tbsp Thai fish sauce (Nam Pla)

1 tbsp dark soy sauce

2 tsp sesame oil

500g pork fillet, cut on the diagonal into long, thin slices

200g rice noodles

100g bean sprouts

1 head of iceberg lettuce, leaves separated and trimmed into cups

2 large handfuls of mint leaves

FOR THE DIPPING SAUCE

2 tbsp caster sugar

3 tbsp Thai fish sauce (Nam Pla)

3 tbsp rice vinegar

1 red chilli, deseeded and finely sliced

1 garlic clove, peeled and finely chopped

Bash together the garlic, lime zest, coriander leaves and stalks and half the spring onions in a pestle and mortar until you have a smooth paste.

Add in the fish sauce, soy sauce and sesame oil and mix through. Place the pork in a bowl and add three quarters of the paste, reserving the rest.

When the pork has marinated (overnight if possible), thread the slices onto skewers and set aside on a plate. Reserve the leftover marinade.

Whisk together all the ingredients for the dipping sauce and place in a serving bowl. Soak the noodles in warm water for a few minutes until tender and then drain in cold water.

Arrange the bean sprouts, noodles, lettuce leaves and herbs in piles on a large serving platter.

Cook the pork over a high heat on a barbecue or a griddle pan for about 2 minutes on either side until cooked through and sizzling. Baste with the leftover marinade to create a sticky coating.

Serve the skewers on the serving platter and allow people to dig in. Wrap the pork in the lettuce cups with the noodles, herbs, bean sprouts and dip in the dipping sauce.

Japanese pot stickers make a wonderful light and aromatic meal. You can easily pick up gyoza wrappers in Asian supermarkets and once you have perfected the technique of assembling the gyoza, it's a simple cooking method. I serve mine with a salty dipping sauce and some wilted bok choy and cashew nuts.

PORK POT STICKERS WITH WARM BOK CHOY & CASHEWS

MAKES 40

FOR THE POT STICKERS

150g pork mince

100g Chinese cabbage, very finely chopped

3 spring onions, trimmed and finely chopped

1 thumb-sized piece of fresh ginger, peeled and finely chopped

1 tbsp rice wine

1 tbsp light soy sauce

1 tsp sesame oil

1 tsp caster sugar

40 gyoza wrappers

FOR THE DIPPING SAUCE

125ml light soy sauce

3 tbsp rice wine

1 tbsp chilli oil

FOR THE DUMPLINGS

1 tbsp sunflower oil

1 tsp sesame oil

FOR THE BOK CHOY

1 tbsp sunflower oil

12 baby bok choy, halved lengthways

75g cashew nuts, toasted

1 tbsp light soy sauce

1 tbsp rice wine

Combine all the ingredients for the pot stickers in a mixing bowl apart from the wrappers and mix through.

Prepare the dipping sauce by whisking all the ingredients in a bowl.

Assemble the dumplings by placing a teaspoon of the meat mix in the centre of each wrapper. Dip your finger in a little cold water and run it around the outside edge of the wrapper. Fold the wrapper over the filling to give a half-moon shape. Before pressing the edges together, pleat the top half from one side to the other, then press down to seal. Alternatively, simply press the edges together to seal.

Repeat the process with the remaining meat and wrappers. The dumplings will sit happily in the fridge, covered, until you are ready to cook them.

To cook the dumplings, heat the sunflower oil in a large high-sided frying pan with a lid over a medium-high heat. Add all the dumplings, pleat-side up, and fry for 3 minutes until they are golden brown underneath. Pour in 100ml of water and the sesame oil, reduce the heat, cover with the lid and allow the dumplings to steam for 2–3 minutes. Remove the lid and turn the heat back up and continue to cook until the water has evaporated. Turn the heat off and cover the pan with the lid while you prepare the bok choy.

Heat the oil in a large wok over a medium-high heat. Stir-fry the bok choy and cashews for 3–4 minutes until the leaves begin to wilt. Sprinkle over the soy sauce and rice wine. Serve the pot stickers with the dipping sauce and wilted bok choy and cashews.

Buttermilk fried chicken is completely trashy and completely delicious. You get a wonderful thick and crispy coating on the chicken and when served with sweet potato fries this is homemade fast food done right. Serve with ketchup and a herby garlic mayonnaise.

BUTTERMILK FRIED CHICKEN WITH SWEET POTATO FRIES

SERVES 4-6

350ml buttermilk

1 whole chicken (approx. 1.2kg), cut into portions (wings, breast, thighs and drumsticks)

Sunflower oil, for frying

100g plain flour

1 tsp dried oregano

1 tsp paprika

2 tsp cayenne pepper

1 tsp garlic powder

Sea salt and ground black pepper

Lime wedges, to serve

Coriander leaves, to serve

FOR THE SWEET POTATO FRIES

1kg sweet potatoes, skin left on and cut into 1cm thick chips

In a bowl, mix together the buttermilk and chicken pieces. Cover and leave in the fridge for 2 hours or overnight, if possible.

When you are ready to cook the chicken, heat a large high-sided frying pan over a medium heat and fill with 3cm of oil. Mix the flour, oregano, paprika, cayenne pepper, garlic powder, sea salt and ground black pepper on a large plate.

Remove the chicken pieces from the buttermilk and dredge in the seasoned flour. Shake off any excess, then place the chicken pieces in the pan to fry. The oil is hot enough when it bubbles vigorously after a sweet potato chip is added. Cook for about 15 minutes on either side until they are cooked through and have a good golden brown colour. Remove from the pan using a slotted spoon and drain on a plate lined with kitchen paper. Keep warm in a low oven while you cook the chips.

Add the sweet potato chips and fry for 6–8 minutes, turning occasionally, until they are crisp and golden. Drain on kitchen paper. Serve the chicken with the sweet potato fries, lime wedges and a few coriander leaves for a rather delicious trashy dinner to share.

If you've never had Jerk chicken before and was wondering what all the fuss was about, well you are in for a treat. The spicy and earthy marinade produces the most delicious tender chicken you will ever have. Served with a cooling and sweet mango salsa this is one of my ultimate summer dishes.

JERK CHICKEN WITH MANGO SALSA

SERVES 4-6

2 Scotch bonnet chillies, deseeded and
  finely chopped

Grated zest and juice of 3 limes

4 garlic cloves, peeled and finely
  chopped

1 thumb-sized piece of fresh ginger,
  peeled and finely chopped

3 tsp allspice

1 tsp ground nutmeg

1 tsp ground cinnamon

1 tsp dried oregano

6 thyme sprigs

2 tbsp honey

6 tbsp tomato ketchup

1 chicken (approx. 1.2kg), cut into
  portions (breasts, wings and legs)

FOR THE MANGO SALSA

2 mangoes, peeled, stones removed and
  roughly chopped in chunks

½ cucumber, centre scooped out and
  cut into cubes

4 spring onions, trimmed and
  finely chopped

1 small red chilli, deseeded and
  finely chopped

Juice of 1 lime

2 tbsp olive oil

Sea salt and ground black pepper

Good handful of coriander leaves,
  roughly chopped

To marinate the chicken, place all the ingredients apart from the chicken in a large resealable bag and mix together. Add the chicken, seal the bag and shake until coated. Leave in the fridge to marinate for at least 2 hours or overnight if you have the time.

Combine all the ingredients for the salsa (except the coriander) in a mixing bowl and season with sea salt and ground black pepper. Mix through the coriander when you're ready to serve.

Remove the chicken from the fridge 30 minutes before you are ready to cook. Get the barbecue to a medium-high heat and cook the chicken pieces for 15 minutes, turning only once during the cooking time, until the chicken is cooked through.

The different pieces will take slightly different cooking times, so a good way to check if they are cooked is to insert a meat thermometer at the thickest part and check that it registers 82°C/180°F for drumsticks and thighs and 76°C/169°F for breasts. Serve the chicken with the mango salsa and some lime wedges and coriander sprigs if you like.

Some of my favourite food nights in have been a hands-on dinner with friends. Homemade pasta is perfect for getting everyone involved. Make the dough and fillings ahead of time and then get everyone to help roll out the dough and assemble the ravioli.

SPRING PEA & RICOTTA RAVIOLI

SERVES 4 (V) (IF VEGETARIAN CHEESE IS USED)

200g tipo 00 pasta flour

1 large egg

3 large egg yolks

Semolina, for dusting

80g butter

Grated zest of 1 lemon

Pecorino cheese, grated, to garnish

FOR THE FILLING

150g ricotta

2 spring onions, trimmed and finely chopped

Large handful of mint leaves, finely chopped

100g pecorino cheese, freshly grated

360g peas, cooked in a little butter for 3 minutes and cooled

Sea salt and ground black pepper

To make the pasta, place the flour, egg and egg yolks in the food processor and pulse until a dough forms. Form it into a ball, cover with cling film and set aside in the fridge.

For the filling, mix together the ricotta, spring onion, mint, pecorino and half the peas in a small bowl and season with sea salt and ground black pepper.

Set the rollers of your pasta machine to the widest setting. Take half the dough and roughly flatten into an oval. Roll the pasta through the rollers five times on each setting until you get to the thinnest one.

When the pasta is as thin as you can get it, lay it out on a work surface dusted with semolina. Cut the pasta into manageable-sized sheets and leave under a damp cloth so they don't dry out.

Taking one pasta sheet at a time, add a teaspoon of the filling at regular intervals, about 5cm apart. Have a cup of water to hand and, using a brush, dampen the edges around the filling, then lay a second sheet of pasta over the top. Gently press down around the edges of the filling to seal, ensuring all the air escapes.

Slice up the ravioli with a sharp knife and place in a large pot of boiling salted water to cook for about 2–3 minutes until the ravioli rise to the top. Drain the cooked ravioli in a colander.

To finish cooking the pasta, place a frying pan over a medium-high heat and add the butter. Melt the butter until it is foaming and turns golden and nutty. Add the lemon zest and then gently toss in the pasta and remaining peas, to cook for no more than 1 minute.

Serve straight away with a little Pecorino to garnish and season with sea salt and ground black pepper.

Fish tacos are a Californian classic, taking inspiration from wonderful Mexican heat and spice. They make a truly different feast to serve for friends. If you don't want to fire up the barbecue, the fish can easily be cooked on a griddle pan.

MEXICAN FISH TACOS

SERVES 6

1 tbsp paprika

1 tsp garlic powder

1 tsp dried oregano

1 tsp cayenne pepper

1 tsp ground cumin

650g cod fillet

1 tbsp sunflower oil

Sour cream, to serve

1 lime, cut into wedges

2 avocados, stoned and finely sliced

Good handful of coriander leaves

1 red onion, peeled and finely sliced

½ head of white cabbage, finely
   shredded

Tabasco sauce

Sea salt

12 x 15cm diameter corn tortillas,
   warmed through

Coriander leaves, to serve

FOR THE SALSA

250g cherry tomatoes, halved

2 spring onions, trimmed and
   finely chopped

1 garlic clove, peeled and finely chopped

Juice of 1 lime

1 tbsp extra virgin olive oil

Sea salt and ground black pepper

To make the salsa, mix together the ingredients in a serving bowl and set aside.

Heat a barbecue or griddle pan to a medium-high heat. Combine the paprika, garlic powder, oregano, cayenne pepper and ground cumin in a bowl. Dust the fish fillet with the spice mix. Brush the grill with the oil and cook the fish for 4–5 minutes on either side until cooked through.

Meanwhile, prepare the accompaniments for the fish by arranging the sour cream, lime wedges, avocado slices, coriander leaves, red onion and cabbage in serving bowls. Squeeze a little lime over the avocado and set everything aside on a large serving platter with a little bottle of Tabasco.

Carefully remove the fish from the pan and break it apart with a fork. Place the flakes in a serving bowl and season with sea salt to taste. Sprinkle with coriander leaves. Add the warm tortillas to the serving platter and assemble little bits of everything in the tortillas. Wrap up and enjoy!

Calzone are basically a folded pizza that you fill with ingredients of your choice. I make mini versions, which are great for serving to friends. Play around with the fillings, but know too that this pizza base recipe also works for pizza and flat bread.

MINI GOAT'S CHEESE, SPINACH & PROSCIUTTO CALZONE

MAKES 8 CALZONE

500g plain flour, plus extra for dusting
2 x 7g sachets of easy blend dried yeast
2 tsp salt
350ml tepid water
2 tsp honey
2 tbsp extra virgin olive oil, plus extra for oiling
4 tbsp semolina, for dusting

FOR THE TOPPINGS

1 x 680g jar of passata
200g mozzarella cheese, cut into slices
2 large handfuls of spinach, softened in a saucepan with a little oil
150g soft goat's cheese
150g prosciutto, thinly sliced

To make the pizza dough, combine the flour, yeast and salt in a large bowl. Make a well in the flour and pour in the water, honey and olive oil. Using your fingertips, slowly bring the flour in from the sides and continue to mix until a rough dough forms.

Turn the dough out on a floured work surface and knead for about 5 minutes. If the dough is too sticky, add a little extra flour until it becomes smooth. Form the dough into a ball and place in an oiled bowl. Cover with a damp tea towel or cling film and set aside in a warm spot for about 45 minutes or until it has doubled in size.

Punch the dough down on a floured work surface, then knead it again for a minute and place back in the bowl to rise for a further 10 minutes.

Preheat the oven to 200°C (400°F), Gas Mark 6 and put a baking sheet or pizza stone in the oven to heat up. Divide the dough into 8 small balls. Dust the work surface with semolina and roll out the balls into 18–20cm diameter rounds as thinly as possible. Spread the base with the passata, then lay on the mozzarella, spinach and goat's cheese and drape over the prosciutto.

Fold the calzone over and crimp the edges to seal. Transfer them to the hot baking sheet or pizza stone and bake in the oven for 10–15 minutes until the crust is golden brown. Serve straight away.

Chimichurri is a tangy and fresh Argentinian sauce. It can be made very easily and is the perfect accompaniment to grilled meat and seafood. This is a mighty feast, which is also quite healthy.

SURF & TURF SALAD

SERVES 6

4 small rib eye steaks

12 Dublin bay prawns, peeled

Sea salt and ground black pepper

1 tbsp rapeseed oil

FOR THE CHIMICHURRI SAUCE

1 onion, peeled and roughly chopped

4 garlic cloves, peeled and chopped

2 handfuls of flat-leaf parsley

1 tsp dried oregano

6 tbsp extra virgin olive oil

3 tbsp red wine vinegar

Pinch of cayenne pepper and sea salt

FOR THE SALAD

3 tbsp extra virgin olive oil

1 tbsp balsamic vinegar

1 garlic clove, peeled and finely chopped

1 tsp Dijon mustard

4 large handfuls of mixed garden
  salad leaves

To make the chimichurri sauce, whizz together the ingredients in a food processor and then transfer it into a bowl. Add a little extra olive oil to loosen if necessary.

Place the steaks on a plate along with the prawns, season them with sea salt and ground black pepper and toss with 2 tablespoons of the chimichurri sauce. Set aside.

In a large bowl, make the salad dressing by whisking together the olive oil, vinegar, garlic and mustard.

Heat the rapeseed oil in a large griddle pan over a high heat and cook the steaks for 3–4 minutes on either side for medium and a little longer if you prefer a more well-done steak. Remove the meat from the pan and allow it to rest on a warmed plate under some foil. Add the prawns to the griddle pan and cook for about 2 minutes on either side.

Slice the steak thinly and add any juices to the dressing. Add the salad leaves to the dressing, toss through and then arrange the leaves on a large serving platter. Top with the steak slices and prawns and then drizzle over the remaining chimichurri sauce. Serve straight away.

I love fuss-free one-tray dinners that can be served straight to the table where people can help themselves. This teriyaki chicken tray bake can be prepared ahead of time and popped in the oven when guests arrive. Then it's just a case of tossing egg noodles through the sauce in the bottom of the pan and adding a few fresh ingredients and you are ready to rock!

SATURDAY NIGHT TERIYAKI CHICKEN

SERVES 6

3 garlic cloves, peeled and finely chopped

1 red chilli, deseeded and finely chopped

1 lime, zest grated and the fruit cut in half

5 tbsp dark soy sauce

1 tbsp dark soft brown sugar

1 tbsp sunflower oil

1 tbsp sesame oil

6 chicken fillets

300g egg noodles, cooked

6 spring onions, trimmed and finely sliced

Small handful of sesame seeds

Good handful of coriander leaves, to garnish

1 red chilli, deseeded and finely sliced, to garnish

In a large bowl, make the marinade for the chicken. Combine the garlic, chilli, lime zest, soy sauce, brown sugar, sunflower oil and sesame oil. Add the chicken and toss to coat. Cover and set aside in the fridge for at least 30 minutes.

Preheat the oven to 200°C (400°F), Gas Mark 6. Pour the chicken and marinade into a roasting tin and place in the oven for 15–20 minutes until the chicken is cooked through, basting with the juices halfway through the cooking time.

Cook the noodles as instructed on the packet, then drain them.

Remove the baking tray from the oven and add the noodles, spring onions and a good squeeze of lime juice. Toss thoroughly until everything is coated. Sprinkle over the sesame seeds and garnish with coriander and red chilli. Serve straight away.

BIG SUNDAY LUNCH

Roast Beef with Salsa Verde 106/
Mini Beef Wellington 108/ Beef
Carpaccio with Beetroot &
Fennel 110/ Lisbeth's Swedish
Salt-Baked Salmon 113/ Sticky
Pork with Crackling & an Apple &
Ginger Sauce 114/ One-tray Roast
Chicken, Potatoes & Asparagus
116/ Ham Hock Terrine 118/
Lamb à la Boulangère 120/ Polenta
Chips with Rosemary Salt 122/
Rosemary-crusted Rack of Lamb
with Crushed Minty Pea Potatoes
124/ Yorkshire Puddings 126/
Barbecued Butterflied Lamb with
Yoghurt & Mint 128/ Sweet &
Sticky Honeyed Duck Legs 130/
Goose Fat Crunchy Roast Potatoes
132/ Thyme Honey & Butter
Roast Carrots 133

When it comes to roast meats for a big Sunday dinner, it's hard to beat the old classic of roast beef. Here it is paired with spiky and fresh salsa verde. Serve with simple sides like roast potatoes, steamed carrots and green beans for a delicious meal.

ROAST BEEF WITH SALSA VERDE

SERVES 6

1 onion, skin left on, cut into
   1cm wide slices
1.5kg rib of beef, rolled
2 tbsp olive oil
1 tbsp dried thyme
1 tbsp English mustard powder
1 tbsp sea salt
1 tbsp ground black pepper

FOR THE GRAVY

100ml red wine
1 heaped tbsp plain flour
150ml beef stock
1 tsp tomato purée
1 tsp Worcestershire sauce

FOR THE SALSA VERDE

6 tbsp extra virgin olive oil
2 tbsp red wine vinegar
1 tsp Dijon mustard
½ tsp sugar
2 garlic cloves
3 anchovy fillets
2 tbsp capers, drained and rinsed
Good handful of flat-leaf parsley
Good handful of basil
Sea salt and ground black pepper

Preheat the oven to 150°C (300°F), Gas Mark 2. Place the onion in the centre of a large roasting tin to act as a trivet and lay the beef on top. Massage the meat with olive oil, then mix the thyme, English mustard powder, sea salt and ground black pepper in a small bowl and pat on the beef. Roast for 1½ hours in the oven for medium rare or until it is cooked to your liking.

Remove from the oven and transfer the meat to a chopping board with thick grooves. Cover with foil to rest for 30 minutes before carving into thin slices. Save the juices in the roasting tin for the gravy.

Meanwhile, make the gravy. Pour any resting juices into the roasting tin the beef was cooked in. Place it over a medium heat and add the red wine, scraping any cooked-on bits from the bottom and sides. Whisk in the flour and then pour in the beef stock, tomato purée and Worcestershire sauce. Continue to cook, whisking regularly until you have a smooth and slightly thickened gravy.

Blitz the ingredients for the salsa verde in a food processor until smooth. Serve the salsa verde drizzled over slices of the beef with steamed carrots, boiled baby potatoes and green beans. Pour over the gravy.

The perfect beef Wellington can be a tricky business, especially when serving to a group who are picky about how their meat is cooked. The solution is mini beef Wellingtons, individually wrapped so your guests can have them cooked exactly how they like.

MINI BEEF WELLINGTON

SERVES 6

6 thick beef fillet steaks with a good
    marbling of fat

Sea salt and ground black pepper

1 tbsp olive oil

English mustard, for brushing the meat

Plain flour, for dusting

500g puff pastry

1 large egg, beaten

FOR THE FILLING

10g dried porcini mushrooms

1 tbsp butter

3 shallots, peeled and finely chopped

300g chestnut mushrooms, finely
    chopped

3 thyme sprigs

100ml brandy

100ml single cream

To make the filling, first soak the porcini mushrooms in boiling water for 10–15 minutes until they are plump and tender. Drain, reserving the soaking liquid, and chop finely.

Melt the butter in a large non-stick frying pan over a medium heat until foaming. Add the shallots and fry for 6 minutes until softened. Stir in the porcini and the chestnut mushrooms together with the thyme and cook for a further 6 minutes until tender. Pour in the mushroom soaking liquid, brandy and cream and simmer until the liquid has reduced and the mixture thickened. Put the filling into a clean bowl and cool completely.

Season the steaks with sea salt and ground black pepper. Wipe the pan with kitchen paper and then place it back over a high heat with a little oil and brown the steaks, in batches if necessary, for about 1 minute on each side. Remove from the heat and rest for at least 30 minutes until completely cool. When cooled, brush each one with mustard.

Preheat the oven to 220°C (425°F), Gas Mark 7. Dust a work surface with flour and roll out the puff pastry into a large rectangle measuring about 45 x 30cm and about 3mm thick. Divide the rectangle into six squares, each one big enough to wrap all the way around each fillet.

Divide the mushroom mixture among the six squares and spread over the pastry, leaving 1cm uncovered all the way around. Place the beef fillet on top. Brush the pastry edges with the egg, then lift the pastry edges over the beef and turn over tucking in the edges neatly. Place the parcels on a baking tray, seam-side down.

Cook in the oven for 15–20 minutes for medium rare or to your liking. Remove from the oven to rest for 5 minutes before serving on warmed plates with steamed greens.

Beef carpaccio has to be one of the easiest starters to prepare and this one looks particularly stunning. To get extra thin slices of beef, cover the cooked fillet in cling film and place it in the freezer for 20 minutes after which time the meat will be firmer and easier to slice.

BEEF CARPACCIO WITH BEETROOT & FENNEL

SERVES 6–8

2 tbsp oil, for frying

900g beef fillet, trimmed

4 tsp coriander seeds

2 tbsp finely chopped rosemary leaves

50g Parmesan cheese shavings, to garnish

FOR THE BEETROOT AND FENNEL

675g raw baby beetroots

3 tbsp olive oil

4 tbsp balsamic vinegar

Sea salt and ground black pepper

1 small fennel bulb, very thinly sliced

50g watercress, well picked over

1 tbsp extra virgin olive oil

½ lemon

FOR THE HORSERADISH DRESSING

4 tbsp grated or creamed horseradish

100g crème fraîche

75ml single cream

2 tbsp snipped chives

Preheat the oven to 220°C (425°F), Gas Mark 7. Remove the beef from the fridge 30 minutes before you intend to use it to allow it to come back to room temperature.

Scrub the beetroots, then trim off the tops. Pat dry with kitchen paper. Place in a roasting tin and drizzle over the olive oil and balsamic vinegar. Season with sea salt and ground black pepper, then cover with foil and roast for 20–30 minutes until tender. They are done when you can pierce them easily with a sharp knife. Leave to cool, then cut each beetroot in half and toss back into the cooking juices to keep them moist.

Smash the coriander seeds in a pestle and mortar until roughly ground and then sprinkle on to a board with the rosemary and half a teaspoon each of salt and pepper. Mix together and then roll the beef all over it, pressing onto the meat to encrust it.

Heat the oil in a large frying pan over a medium-high heat until it is smoking hot. Add the meat to the pan and sear for about 6 minutes until well browned all over and slightly crisp, turning regularly. Remove from the heat and leave to rest on a board, uncovered, for at least 20 minutes.

recipe continues…

BEEF CARPACCIO WITH BEETROOT & FENNEL

Meanwhile, make the horseradish dressing. Place the horseradish, crème fraîche, cream and chives in a bowl and mix well to combine, then season to taste. Add a few tablespoons of water to loosen the sauce, if needed.

When the beef has rested, slice it as thinly as you can (see the freezing suggestion in the recipe introduction) and arrange in an overlapping layer on large plates. Scatter over the roasted beetroots and drizzle some of the beetroot cooking juices on top, then dribble over the dressing.

Dress the fennel and watercress with the extra virgin olive oil. Squeeze over lemon juice and then scatter the salad over the finished plates. Garnish with the Parmesan shavings, a good dollop of crème fraîche and add a grinding of black pepper to serve.

When I visit Sweden, more often than not we visit the rather amazing Lisbeth, a whirlwind of a woman who loves to eat, drink and be merry. Novelty or not, this salt-baked salmon is one of her dinner party dishes and it's something rather impressive served to a table of hungry guests.

LISBETH'S SWEDISH SALT-BAKED SALMON

SERVES 8

1.5kg sea salt
4 egg whites
Grated zest and juice of 1 lemon
1.8kg salmon fillet, skin on
1 tsp black peppercorns, lightly crushed
2 large handfuls of dill leaves, chopped
Lemon wedges, to serve

Preheat the oven to 180°C (350°F), Gas Mark 4. Mix the sea salt, egg whites and lemon juice in a large bowl. Spread one-third of the sea salt mixture on the base of a large roasting tin. Lay the salmon on top, then spread over the peppercorns, dill and lemon zest. Cover with the remaining salt mix and cook in the oven for about 45 minutes until the salmon is cooked through.

Remove from the oven and push the salt topping off the fish exposing the flesh. Tumble in a few lemon wedges and serve straight to the table with steamed greens and boiled baby potatoes.

I have pork crackling-filled dreams and when they all get too much this is the dish I turn to in order to satisfy my subconscious. Both apple and ginger work incredibly well with pork and the sweet sauce here is a wonderful accompaniment.

STICKY PORK WITH CRACKLING & AN APPLE & GINGER SAUCE

SERVES 6

1 large onion, skin left on, cut
    into slices

1.5kg pork loin, boned and rolled
    with the rind scored

1 tbsp sunflower oil

Sea salt and ground black pepper

1 tbsp honey

¼ tsp Chinese five-spice powder

2 tbsp plain flour

350ml cider

FOR THE APPLE AND GINGER SAUCE

1 tbsp butter

1 onion, peeled and finely chopped

2 cooking apples, peeled, cored and
    finely chopped

1 thumb-sized piece of fresh ginger,
    peeled and finely grated

1 tbsp caster sugar

Preheat the oven to 240°C (475°F), Gas Mark 9. Place the onion in the centre of a roasting tin to act as a trivet and lay the pork on top. Drizzle with a little oil and season with sea salt and ground black pepper. Place in the oven to cook for 20 minutes, then reduce the heat to 180°C (350°F), Gas Mark 4 and cook for a further 1½ hours.

Meanwhile, prepare the apple and ginger sauce. Melt the butter in a saucepan over a medium-high heat until it is foaming. Add the onion and fry for about 6 minutes until the onion has softened. Add the apples, ginger and sugar to the pan and cook until the apples are soft and mushy. Mash all the ingredients together until you have a smooth sauce. Season to taste and keep warm.

Remove the pork from the oven and mix together the honey and five-spice powder. Brush the mixture over the pork crackling and return the joint to the oven for a further 5 minutes. Remove the meat from the oven, transfer it to a chopping board with grooves, then cover with foil and allow to rest for 30 minutes.

Spoon off most of the fat from the roasting tin and place it over a medium heat. Whisk in the flour, then pour in the cider and bring it to a steady simmer until the sauce thickens slightly, continually whisking until smooth. Pour any meat resting juices back into the gravy. Strain it through a sieve and transfer to a gravy boat.

Carve the pork into generous slices and serve with the apple and ginger sauce and the gravy together with steamed greens and roast potatoes.

When choosing a chicken for roasting, make sure to choose a bird that's nice and plump, which looks healthy with no blemishes or imperfections and has nice unbroken skin. You can use whatever veggies are in season to pop in the tray alongside the chicken. Vegetables like beetroot, squash and tomatoes are all ideal additions. This is a great repertoire recipe that you can produce at the drop of a hat and with little thought!

ONE-TRAY ROAST CHICKEN, POTATOES & ASPARAGUS

SERVES 4

800g new baby potatoes, halved

1 garlic bulb, cloves separated and skins left on

1 lemon, sliced

Handful of thyme sprigs

3 tbsp rapeseed oil

Sea salt and ground black pepper

1 whole chicken (approx. 1.5kg)

Large knob of butter

125ml white wine

Large bunch of asparagus, woody ends snapped off

Handful of flat-leaf parsley, finely chopped

Preheat the oven to 200°C (400°F), Gas Mark 6. Put the new potatoes, garlic cloves and lemon slices into a large roasting tin. Scatter with the thyme sprigs and drizzle with the oil. Season well and toss to combine.

Remove the string trussing the chicken and gently loosen the skin on the chicken's breasts to form a pocket, being careful not to tear it. Push a little butter under the skin, then spread more over the outside. Season with sea salt and ground black pepper. Put the chicken on top of the potatoes, then roast for 1¼ hours or until cooked. Transfer the chicken to a warmed plate, cover it with foil and leave it to rest somewhere warm for 10 minutes.

Pour the wine into the roasting tin, then add the asparagus and mix everything together so the vegetables are coated in the wine and chicken juices. Return the tray to the oven and roast for a further 10 minutes until the potatoes are tender. Remove from the oven and then stir the parsley through the potatoes and asparagus and serve alongside the carved chicken.

I have a special place in my heart for ham hocks. Certainly not the most attractive ingredient to hold a fondness for, but I put it down to my inner cheapskate. I love the idea that for very little money you can produce something delicious. This ham hock recipe doesn't use gelatin, but if you prefer a firmer setting you could add a leaf of gelatin to the cooking liquid once the ham hocks are cooked. You can also make the terrine in individual Kilner jars to serve.

HAM HOCK TERRINE

SERVES 8

4kg ham hock (about 2 large or
    4 smaller ham hocks)
8 whole black peppercorns
1 bay leaf
Small handful of thyme
2 carrots, peeled and cut into
    small cubes
1 onion, peeled and roughly cut
    into pieces
3 celery stalks, trimmed and cut into
    small cubes
60ml white wine vinegar
Generous handful of flat-leaf parsley,
    finely chopped

Place the ham hocks in a large pot with the peppercorns, bay leaf and thyme. Cover with water and bring to the boil. Reduce the heat, cover with a lid and let it simmer for 3 hours or until the meat is incredibly tender and falling off the bone. You can check this using a fork.

About 45 minutes before the meat is done, add the vegetables and cook until they are tender. When they are cooked, remove the vegetables from the liquid with a slotted spoon and set aside. Remove the ham hocks from the liquid once they are tender and set aside to cool. Pour out the cooking liquid leaving 1.2 litres in the pot.

Add the vinegar to the remaining cooking liquid and bring to a steady boil for about 1 hour or until it has reduced by at least half. You will need roughly 600ml to set the terrine.

When the ham hocks have cooled, remove the skin and shred the meat. Place the shredded meat in a bowl with the parsley and toss until completely coated.

Line a 900g loaf tin or terrine mould with two layers of cling film, leaving extra over the sides. Layer the shredded meat and reserved vegetables into the mould and then press down firmly. Slowly pour some of the reduced cooking liquid into the terrine, allowing it to work its way through all the layers. Cover with a little more cling film and leave in the fridge to set overnight.

To serve, turn the terrine out on to a chopping board and peel away the cling film. Dip a knife in boiling water and cut the terrine into slices. Serve with garden leaves and a tangy white wine vinaigrette.

Two wonderful ingredients at their very best are the heroes of this traditionally French recipe. The lamb sits on a rack to cook above a tray of thinly sliced potatoes, which soak up all those wonderful juices. You are left with beautifully cooked lamb and the most incredible potatoes, the ingredients for a perfect Sunday lunch.

LAMB À LA BOULANGÈRE

SERVES 6

2kg leg of lamb

Olive oil, for rubbing

Sea salt and ground black pepper

4 rosemary sprigs

3 garlic cloves, peeled and sliced

1.2kg waxy potatoes, thinly sliced

1 large onion, finely sliced

A few thyme sprigs, leaves picked

1 bay leaf

500ml beef or lamb stock

Preheat the oven to 220°C (425°F), Gas Mark 7. Using a small sharp knife, poke holes all over the lamb. Rub with olive oil and season generously with sea salt and ground black pepper and stud with rosemary and garlic. Place in a roasting tin and cook in the oven for 25 minutes.

Meanwhile, mix together the potatoes with the onion, thyme and bay leaf in a bowl and season with sea salt and ground black pepper.

After 25 minutes, remove the roasting tin from the oven. Transfer the lamb to a warmed plate and tumble the potatoes into the roasting tin, toss to coat and then pour in the stock. Place the roasting tin back in the oven on the bottom shelf and place the lamb directly on the middle shelf directly over the potatoes. This allows the lamb juices to drip down into the potatoes as they cook.

Cook for about 50 minutes for a medium-cooked leg of lamb, or cook until the meat is to your liking. Serve the lamb in slices with the potatoes and some dressed salad leaves.

Polenta chips are an extra special little side dish that works perfectly with meat. The addition here of nigella seeds adds a wonderful onion taste and texture.

POLENTA CHIPS WITH ROSEMARY SALT

SERVES 6-8

Sunflower oil, for oiling
1 litre chicken stock
250g packet of instant polenta
1 tbsp nigella seeds
50g Parmesan cheese, very finely grated
Sunflower oil, for frying

FOR THE ROSEMARY SALT

2 large rosemary sprigs, leaves picked
    and finely chopped
1 tbsp sea salt

Grease a 22 x 30cm baking tin with oil and set aside.

In a large saucepan, bring the chicken stock to the boil. Using a whisk, gradually add the polenta, whisking until it is all incorporated. Cook gently for about 2 minutes until the polenta is soft or according to the packet instructions. Mix through the nigella seeds, then pour the polenta into the prepared tin, allow to cool and cover. Set aside to set for 3–4 hours or overnight.

When you are ready to make the chips, slice the polenta into 2cm-thick chips. Sprinkle with Parmesan cheese and gently toss to coat.

Pour the sunflower oil into a high-sided non-stick saucepan to about 2cm deep and heat it over a medium-high heat. Working in batches, fry the polenta chips for about 5 minutes until they are golden brown, turning occasionally. Set aside on a plate lined with kitchen paper and keep warm in the oven until you are ready to serve.

Alternatively, drizzle with olive oil and bake on a flat baking tray in an oven at 200°C (400°F), Gas Mark 6 for 30 minutes until golden, turning occasionally.

To make the rosemary salt, bash the rosemary in a pestle and mortar and then stir through the sea salt. Serve with the polenta chips.

This is a total showstopper of a spring Sunday lunch. It's ideal for a crowd and really doesn't take too much effort for truly impressive results. For me, it's the combination of sweet lamb and popping peas, fresh mint and buttery potatoes that makes this totally delicious family food.

ROSEMARY-CRUSTED RACK OF LAMB WITH CRUSHED MINTY PEA POTATOES

SERVES 4

100g white bread, broken into chunks
3 thyme sprigs, leaves picked
2 rosemary sprigs, leaves picked
Good handful of flat-leaf parsley leaves
2 garlic cloves, peeled and roughly chopped
Sea salt and ground black pepper
2 x 6-bone lean racks of lamb, French trimmed
60g butter
3 tbsp Dijon mustard
1 heaped tsp plain flour
350ml lamb or beef stock

FOR THE CRUSHED MINTY PEA POTATOES

1kg baby potatoes, skin on
500g frozen peas
Good handful of mint leaves, finely chopped
6 spring onions, trimmed and finely chopped
75g butter

Preheat the oven to 220°C (425°F), Gas Mark 7. In a small food processor, blitz together the bread, herbs and garlic and season to taste. Also season the lamb racks generously with salt and pepper and set aside.

Melt the butter in a large frying pan over a medium-high heat until it is foaming. Add the lamb and sear it for about 4 minutes on either side until you have good colour. Transfer the lamb to a plate and allow it to cool slightly for 10 minutes.

Cover the fatty side of the meat with Dijon mustard and pat on the herby breadcrumbs to coat. Place the meat in a roasting tin and cook for 15 minutes for rare or until it is to your liking. Remove from the oven, transfer to a carving board and cover with foil until you are ready to serve.

Place the roasting tin with the juices over a medium-high heat and whisk in the flour until combined and then pour in the stock. Simmer until the sauce thickens slightly.

For the crushed minty pea potatoes, put the potatoes in a large pot of cold water and place it over a high heat. Bring to the boil and then simmer for 10–15 minutes until the potatoes are tender when pierced with a fork. About 3 minutes before they are ready, add the peas to the water.

Drain the potatoes and peas into a colander and then return them to the pot along with the mint, spring onions, butter and a generous seasoning of sea salt and ground black pepper. Using a potato masher, gently crush the peas and potatoes together leaving lots of nice chunks.

Slice the lamb and serve alongside the mushy minty potatoes and peas and drizzle over the sauce.

I have to confess that I had never had a Yorkshire pudding until a couple of years ago. Our family roast dinner just didn't include these little light and golden dumplings, but boy have we been missing out! A great addition to any roast dinner, they are wonderfully simple to make.

YORKSHIRE PUDDINGS

MAKES 12 YORKSHIRE PUDDINGS (V)
Sunflower oil, for oiling
120g strong white flour
Pinch of salt
4 large eggs
180ml milk

Preheat the oven to 220°C (425°F), Gas Mark 7. Drizzle about 1 teaspoon of the oil into each hole of a 12-hole non-stick muffin tin and place in the oven while you prepare the batter.

Whisk the flour, salt and eggs in a large jug until smooth and then add the milk slowly, mixing until it is all combined and you have a thin batter.

Remove the muffin tin from the oven and, working quickly and carefully, pour the batter evenly among all 12 holes.

Place the tin back in the oven immediately and cook for 15–20 minutes or until the puddings are puffed up and golden brown. Serve straight away alongside any roast dinner.

If you've never barbecued with lamb before, you are totally missing out on one of my favourite flavours. The longer the lamb is left to marinate, the more tender it becomes. The lamb can also be cooked in a hot oven for the same amount of time.

BARBECUED BUTTERFLIED LAMB WITH YOGHURT & MINT

SERVES 4-6

2kg leg of lamb, butterflied

250ml natural Greek yoghurt

Grated zest and juice of 1 lemon

5 spring onions, trimmed and
   finely chopped

6 garlic cloves, peeled and finely chopped

2 generous handfuls of mint leaves,
   roughly chopped

Sea salt and ground black pepper

Place all the ingredients for the lamb into a large resealable bag and seal. Give it a good shake so that everything is combined and the lamb is completely covered in the dark mixture. Put it in the fridge to marinate for 2–6 hours or overnight.

Remove the lamb bag from the fridge about 40 minutes before you are ready to cook it. Thread two large metal skewers across the lamb to make it easier to transfer to the barbecue and also to turn. Scrape off the marinade, transfer it to a small saucepan and simmer until reduced by half. Set aside.

To cook the lamb on a gas barbecue, bring it to a high heat and sear the lamb on either side for about 4 minutes, then turn the heat right down low, cover with a lid and cook for about 40 minutes until a meat thermometer registers 54°C/130°F (for medium rare), turning the meat halfway through the cooking time.

To cook on a charcoal barbecue, prepare the grill by placing a double layer of coals on one side of the barbecue and a single layer on the other. In this way, you can sear the lamb on the double-layered side and then move it to the side with the single layer to cook for the longer cooking time. Follow the same cooking times and temperatures. If the lamb blackens too much, simply place it on a sheet of foil.

When the lamb is cooked, transfer the joint to a carving board to catch the juices, cover it with foil and allow to rest for about 15 minutes. Pour the resting juices into the reduced marinade and warm through. Slice the lamb thinly and serve with the sauce and some couscous.

I love the simplicity of this dish as it's all about taking a few simple ingredients and combining them to make something rather special. It also makes a wonderful dish to serve to a crowd as the duck legs will sit in the warm oven until you are ready for them.

SWEET & STICKY HONEYED DUCK LEGS

SERVES 6

6 duck legs
Sea salt and ground black pepper
800g parsnips, peeled and quartered
    lengthways
1 tbsp olive oil
6 tbsp honey
160ml cider vinegar

Preheat the oven to 240°C (475°F), Gas Mark 9. Season the duck legs generously with sea salt and ground black pepper and place them in a large roasting tin. Put them in the oven and prepare the parsnips.

Bring a large pot of water to the boil and parboil the parsnips for 5 minutes. Drain the parsnips, return them to the pot and toss a little to rough up the edges. Place the parsnips among the hot duck legs and drizzle with the oil and any of the duck fat that has been rendered. Return the tin to the oven and reduce the temperature to 200°C (400°F), Gas Mark 6. Cook for 50 minutes– 1 hour until the meat is just about falling off the bone.

While the duck is roasting, combine the honey and vinegar in a saucepan and allow the sauce to simmer until the liquid has reduced by half. Set aside until you are ready to serve.

When the duck is cooked, place each duck leg on a warmed plate with the parsnips, drizzle with the sticky honey sauce and serve dressed with some winter leaves.

These have to be the most amazing potatoes and they are just the way I like them – crispy and crunchy on the outside and light and fluffy on the inside. It's really worth getting some goose fat as it imparts wonderful flavour. Toss in a few unpeeled garlic cloves and rosemary or thyme sprigs for even more flavour.

GOOSE FAT CRUNCHY ROAST POTATOES

SERVES 6

100g goose fat
1.4kg potatoes, peeled and quartered
Sea salt

Preheat the oven to 220°C (425°F), Gas Mark 7 and place the goose fat in a roasting tin and then put the tin into the oven.

Place the potatoes in a large pot and fill up with water until covered. Cover with a lid and bring the pot to the boil over a high heat, then reduce the heat and simmer for 7–10 minutes. The potatoes should be cooked on the outer edge but still raw on the inside – you can check this by piercing with a fork.

Drain the potatoes and then return them to the pot. Place the lid on and give a gentle shake to lightly fluff the edges. Then tumble the potatoes into the hot goose fat and toss each one to coat before sprinkling with a generous amount of sea salt. Roast for about 35 minutes until golden and crisp.

These sweet roast carrots caramelised with honey butter and thyme are one of my favourite ways to enjoy them – the perfect accompaniment to any big Sunday lunch.

THYME HONEY & BUTTER ROAST CARROTS

SERVES 4 (V)

16 small carrots, peeled
2 tbsp olive oil
Sea salt and ground black pepper
2 tbsp butter, softened
2 tbsp honey
3 thyme sprigs, leaves picked

Preheat the oven to 200°C (400°F), Gas Mark 6. Place the carrots in a roasting tin and drizzle with a little olive oil and sprinkle with sea salt and ground black pepper. Place in the oven to cook for 30 minutes.

Remove from the oven, give a little shake and dot with small knobs of butter, drizzle with honey and sprinkle over the thyme. Return the tin to the oven for a further 15–20 minutes until the carrots are tender and caramelised. Serve straight away.

WEEKEND BRUNCH

PepperPot Roast Pear, Montgomery Cheese & Bacon Sandwich 136/ La-Style Bacon, Avocado, Lettuce & Tomato Sandwich 138/ Strawberry & Mascarpone Cheese Belgian Waffle Stacks 139/ Eggs Benedict 140/ Caramelised Banana Pancakes 142/ Hole In The Bread Breakfast Eggs 144/ Kedgeree 145/ Wild Honey Omelette Arnold Bennett 146/ Brioche French Toast with Berries & Nutella 148/ Scrambled Egg Croissants 150/ Crusty Croque Madam 152

One of my favourite places to have breakfast or lunch in Dublin is the PepperPot café. This sandwich could quite easily go down as my desert island dish. Sweet sticky pears, salty, crisp bacon and light and crusty batch bread. Pure genius and perfect for the morning after.

PEPPERPOT ROAST PEAR, MONTGOMERY CHEESE & BACON SANDWICH

SERVES 2

3 pears, peeled and cut into eighths

1 tbsp olive oil

2 tbsp honey

1 tbsp balsamic vinegar

6 slices of dry cure bacon

2 tbsp mayonnaise

4 slices of batch white bread

100g Montgomery Cheddar cheese, cut into thick slices

FOR THE SALAD

1 tbsp balsamic vinegar

3 tbsp extra virgin olive oil

1 tsp wholegrain mustard

Sea salt and ground black pepper

Large handful of salad leaves

Preheat the oven to 200°C (400°F), Gas Mark 6. Toss the pears in a large roasting tin with the olive oil, honey and balsamic vinegar. Cook the pears in the oven for 35 minutes until tender when pierced with a fork. Turn occasionally with a fork to prevent them from sticking. Remove and set aside to cool slightly.

Cook the bacon under a hot grill on both sides until crisp.

For the salad, mix the vinegar, extra virgin oil and mustard in a bowl and season with sea salt and ground black pepper. Add the salad leaves and toss to coat.

Spread a little mayo on each slice of bread and assemble the sandwich by layering up the leaves, bacon, cooked pears and cheese. Cut in half and serve straight away.

Sometimes the best moments in food come from the simplest things. This is one of my favourite sandwiches and the addition of avocado was something I picked up on a recent trip to LA.

LA-STYLE BACON, AVOCADO, LETTUCE & TOMATO SANDWICH

SERVES 2

6 rashers of streaky bacon
4 slices of sourdough bread, toasted
3 tbsp mayonnaise
1 Baby Gem lettuce, leaves separated
1 large beef tomato, sliced
1 large avocado, stoned and sliced
Sea salt and ground black pepper

Cook the bacon under a hot grill until crispy.

Assemble the sandwich by spreading the sourdough toast with mayo and then layering up the lettuce, tomato, avocado and season with sea salt and ground black pepper and finally add the bacon.

Devour straight away.

One of my first kitchen-related presents was a waffle maker from my aunt. It meant that my family and friends were subjected to sweet waffles every time there was a family gathering and dessert time rolled around. These strawberry and mascarpone Belgian waffles make a treat of a breakfast and can also be served as a dessert.

STRAWBERRY & MASCARPONE CHEESE BELGIAN WAFFLE STACKS

MAKES 8–10 WAFFLES (V)
225g plain flour
50g caster sugar
2 tsp baking powder
200ml milk
2 large eggs, separated
75g butter, melted
1 tsp vanilla extract

FOR THE TOPPING
250g strawberries
100g mascarpone cheese
2 tbsp strawberry jam, loosened
  with a little boiling water

To make the waffle batter, put all the dry ingredients into a large mixing bowl. Measure the milk in a jug and stir in the egg yolks, melted butter and vanilla extract. In a separate bowl, whisk the egg whites until soft white peaks form.

Make a well in the dry ingredients and pour in the milk and egg yolks. Mix to make a smooth batter and then fold through the egg whites.

Transfer ladlesful of the batter to a waffle iron and cook for 3–4 minutes until golden brown. Serve with strawberries and a dollop of mascarpone cheese and drizzle with strawberry jam.

Eggs Benedict has to be one of my ultimate treat breakfasts. Runny poached eggs with salty crisp bacon on top of a soft toasted English muffin, all coated in a tangy rich Hollandaise sauce — true perfection!

EGGS BENEDICT

SERVES 2–4

6 rashers of smoked streaky bacon
Pinch of salt
1 tsp white wine vinegar
4 large eggs
2 English muffins, split and toasted
Butter, for the muffins
Small handful of chives, snipped

FOR THE HOLLANDAISE SAUCE

2 large egg yolks
150g butter, cold and cut into cubes
Juice of ½ lemon

Cook the bacon under a hot grill until it is crisp.

To make the hollandaise sauce, place the egg yolks in a large heatproof bowl over a pan of gently simmering water. Whisk the yolks and slowly add the butter, bit by bit after each one melts, whisking continuously until it is completely combined and the sauce has thickened. Add the lemon juice and stir through. Turn off the heat, but keep the sauce warm over the pan of water.

To cook the eggs, bring a saucepan of water to the boil and add the salt and vinegar. Swirl the water with a tablespoon and then gently crack an egg into the centre. Cook the egg at a very gentle simmer for 3–4 minutes for the yolk to still be runny. Remove with a slotted spoon and place them in iced water to stop them cooking any further. Repeat with the remaining eggs. Just before serving, reheat the eggs in warm water for 1 minute.

Butter the muffins and assemble the eggs Benedict by placing a few slices of bacon and an egg on each half and then top with the warm hollandaise sauce. Sprinkle over the chives and serve straight away.

I love making American-style pancakes for breakfast and this version is particularly delicious. It is perfect for special occasions!

CARAMELISED BANANA PANCAKES

MAKES ABOUT 8–10 PANCAKES (V)

200g plain flour
2 tsp baking powder
Pinch of sea salt
½ tsp ground cinnamon
220ml milk
2 large eggs
A little butter, melted
50g toasted hazelnuts, roughly chopped

FOR THE CARAMELISED BANANAS

75g butter, plus a knob
100g golden syrup
8 mini bananas, halved lengthways
1 tbsp caster sugar

To make the pancake batter, put all the dry ingredients into a large mixing bowl. Measure the milk in a jug and add the eggs. Whisk lightly to combine, then add the liquid to the dry ingredients and mix until blended and you have a thick batter. Set aside in the fridge.

For the bananas, put the butter and golden syrup into a small saucepan and bring to the boil. Reduce the heat and allow the mixture to simmer and bubble for about 3 minutes until the sauce thickens. Remove the pan from the heat.

Coat the bananas in a little sugar and melt the knob of butter in a large frying pan over a medium heat. Add the banana slices and cook them on all sides until golden. Pour over the butter and golden syrup sauce and stir gently to combine. Set aside.

To cook the pancakes, brush a warm frying pan with a little melted butter and pour in a small ladleful of the batter. The pancakes should each be about 10cm wide. Allow them to cook until little bubbles start to appear and the edges become a little dry and then turn over to cook for about a minute until golden brown.

Serve immediately on warmed plates with the caramelised bananas and sauce on top, sprinkled with the toasted hazelnuts.

These were my Dad's speciality when we were growing up, and I think it's the novelty of them that kept us asking for them again and again.

HOLE IN THE BREAD BREAKFAST EGGS

SERVES 2 (V)

2 slices of bread

A good knob of butter

1 tbsp olive oil

2 large eggs

A little sweet chilli sauce, to serve

3 spring onions, trimmed and finely
   sliced, to garnish

Cut a circle out of the centre of each slice of bread using a pint glass or a straight-sided cutter. Melt the butter with the olive oil in a large non-stick frying pan over a medium-high heat. Put the bread in the pan and fry until golden.

Turn the bread over and crack the eggs into the holes and continue to fry until the eggs turn from translucent to white. You can speed this up by covering the pan. Serve straight away on warmed plates and drizzle with a little sweet chilli sauce and garnish with spring onion.

This wonderful spiced rice and egg dish from colonial India makes for a rather different breakfast. Keep an eye out for undyed smoked haddock. Many fishmongers and supermarkets now stock it and the flavour is far superior.

KEDGEREE

SERVES 2

1 tbsp butter, plus a little extra
1 onion, peeled and finely chopped
250g basmati rice, washed and drained
1 tbsp garam masala
1 heaped tsp turmeric
600ml chicken stock
Sea salt and ground black pepper
2 small smoked haddock fillets, skinned
Small handful of flat-leaf parsley, chopped
3 soft-boiled eggs, shelled and halved
Lemon wedges, to serve

Melt the butter in a high-sided saucepan over a medium heat until it is foaming and golden. Add the onion, reduce the heat and sweat gently for about 8 minutes until is has softened. Add the rice, garam masala and turmeric and cook gently, tossing until completely coated in the onion and butter for 2 minutes.

Add the stock and stir through. Cover with a lid and allow to cook gently for 15 minutes until all the liquid has been absorbed. About 5 minutes before the rice is cooked, stir in sea salt and ground black pepper as necessary and lay the haddock fillets over the top, dotting them with a little extra butter. Continue cooking with the lid on until the rice is tender, then gently fork the fish through the rice.

Serve generous portions on warmed plates topped with parsley, soft-boiled eggs and wedges of lemon.

This treat of a breakfast recipe comes from the charming Wild Honey Inn, run by Aidan McGrath and his wife Kate Sweeney, deep in the heart of the spectacular Burren on the west coast of Ireland. It makes a rich and creamy omelette with a wonderful deep flavour from the smoked fish.

WILD HONEY OMELETTE ARNOLD BENNETT

MAKES 1

200ml whipping cream

2 large eggs

Sea salt and ground black pepper

1 tbsp sunflower oil

1 tbsp butter

50g Gruyère cheese, diced

50g smoked haddock, skinned and diced

3 tbsp grated Parmesan cheese

1 large egg yolk

Watercress, to garnish

Whip up half the cream and set aside in the fridge. Heat the grill to high.

In a separate bowl, whisk the whole eggs with the rest of the cream and season with sea salt and ground black pepper.

Heat the oil in a frying pan over a medium-high heat, then add the butter and melt it until it is foaming. Working quickly, pour the omelette mix into the pan, stirring slightly. Add the Gruyère and smoked haddock and mix them through. Cook for a further minute or so to allow the egg to set.

Mix together the Parmesan cheese, egg yolk and reserved chilled whipped cream in a bowl. With a small spoon spread the mix over the top of the omelette and then place it under the hot grill until it turns golden.

Serve on a plate with the watercress to garnish. Enjoy with multigrain toasted bread for breakfast.

This is definitely not an everyday breakfast, but for special occasions it makes a wonderful celebration breakfast.

BRIOCHE FRENCH TOAST WITH BERRIES & NUTELLA

SERVES 2 (V)
2 large eggs
60ml milk
1 tsp vanilla extract
Nutella, for filling
4 large slices of brioche
1 tbsp softened butter
Icing sugar, for dusting

FOR THE SWEET BERRY SAUCE
100g frozen berries
1 tbsp caster sugar

To make the sweet berry sauce, place the berries and caster sugar in a small saucepan with 50ml of water. Bring the mixture to a steady simmer and cook until the berries are soft. Blitz with a hand-held blender or mash with a fork.

In a large flat dish, whisk together the eggs, milk and vanilla extract. Spread the Nutella on each slice of brioche and then make two sandwiches.

Melt the butter in a large frying pan over a medium-high heat until it is foaming. Soak the brioche sandwiches in the eggs and milk and place straight in the pan to cook for 2–3 minutes on either side until golden.

Remove from the pan and slice in two. Place on two warmed serving plates and drizzle with the berry sauce and dust over the icing sugar.

My regular breakfast is scrambled egg on toast, but for special occasions these scrambled egg croissants with rocket and goat's cheese are a real treat.

SCRAMBLED EGG CROISSANTS

SERVES 2 (V)

2 large croissants

2 handfuls of rocket leaves

4 large eggs

Sea salt and ground black pepper

1 tsp softened butter

100g soft goat's cheese

A few chives, snipped, to serve

Slice open the croissants and fill them with a generous amount of rocket leaves. Set aside.

In a small non-stick saucepan, whisk the eggs together until combined. Place the saucepan over a medium-low heat and, using a wooden spoon, slowly pull the eggs towards the centre. Keep the mixture moving until you have really creamy scrambled eggs. Make sure not to overcook the eggs – take them off the heat while they are still slightly runny and creamy.

Season with sea salt and black pepper and stir through the butter and goat's cheese. Serve in the open croissants with an extra sprinkle of black pepper and a few snips of chives.

A good croque madam really is a thing of beauty, but I have a dislike for the overly sweet sliced white bread you find in Parisien cafés. You will have to forgive me for a slight variation on a classic here, but I like the crunch from the toasted sourdough bread and rather than serving a fried egg on top, I like mine on the plate so I can dip the croque madam soldiers in.

CRUSTY CROQUE MADAM

SERVES 2

4 slices sourdough bread

2 tsp Dijon mustard

200g sliced cooked ham

150g Gruyère cheese, grated

1 tbsp olive oil

2 large eggs

Good handful of chives, snipped

FOR THE WHITE SAUCE

2 tbsp butter

2 tbsp plain flour

200ml milk

Pinch of grated nutmeg

Sea salt and ground black pepper

Toast the sourdough slices under a medium-high grill until just golden. Remove and set aside and increase the grill to high.

For the white sauce, melt the butter in a small saucepan until it is foaming and then add the flour, mixing with a wooden spoon until a roux has formed. Keep beating the roux over the heat for 1 minute until you get a smell of cooked pastry. Add the milk and nutmeg and season with sea salt and ground black pepper. Whisk through until you have a smooth mix, then continue to cook over the heat until you have a thick white sauce.

Assemble the croques by spreading a little Dijon mustard on each slice of sourdough toast, add the ham and then a generous amount of white sauce. Top with the Gruyère cheese and place it under the hot grill for about 5 minutes until the cheese is golden and bubbling.

While the bread is cooking, heat the oil in a non-stick frying pan over a medium-high heat. Add the eggs and fry them for about 3 minutes until cooked. Place each croque on a warmed plate with an egg on the side. Serve with a sprinkle of chives and dig in.

DESSERTS & SWEET TREATS

This rich dark chocolate ganache tart makes a wonderful after-dinner treat with coffee. I finish mine off with a dusting of gold powder, which you can buy online or in speciality baking shops.

MILLIONAIRE CHOCOLATE GANACHE TART

SERVES 6–8 (V)

FOR THE PASTRY

150g plain flour, plus extra for dusting

75g cold butter, diced and chilled

25g caster sugar

1 large egg, beaten

FOR THE FILLING

240ml double cream

200g dark chocolate (70% cocoa solids), finely chopped

75g caster sugar

Gold powder, to decorate (optional)

To make the pastry, rub the flour and butter together in a bowl with your fingertips until the mixture resembles rough breadcrumbs. Stir through the sugar and a little beaten egg until the mix comes together to form a ball. Press it into a flat oval, cover with cling film and place in the fridge to rest for 30 minutes.

Preheat the oven to 180°C (350°F), Gas Mark 4. Dust a work surface with a little flour and roll out the pastry to 3mm in thickness and large enough to fit a 20cm diameter, 4cm deep fluted tart tin with a removable base. Line the tin with the pastry and press it into the sides before trimming the edges. As you line the tin, if the pastry crumbles, don't panic, just patch it together.

Prick the base with a fork all over and line with foil, shiny side down, and fill with baking beans. Place the pastry shell in the oven to blind bake for about 15 minutes until the pastry is a light golden brown. Remove the tin from the oven, lift out the foil and beans and cook for a further 6–8 minutes until cooked through and lightly golden. Remove the tin from the oven again and allow it to cool on a wire rack.

Prepare the filling by placing all the ingredients in a heatproof bowl over a pan of simmering water. Mix until smooth and then pour into the cooled pastry case. Allow to set in the fridge for 1 hour, before dusting with gold powder, if using, and serving in generous slices with a scoop of ice cream and cups of coffee.

This slightly unusual rough and ready pie uses crème fraîche and raspberries as its filling and makes a wonderful summer-time dessert.

RASPBERRY GODDESS PIE

SERVES 6–8 (V)

225g plain flour
125g caster sugar
125g cold butter
1 tsp vanilla extract
1 tsp baking powder
250g raspberries
200ml crème fraîche
Handful of raspberries, to decorate
Small handful of mint sprigs,
    to decorate
Vanilla ice cream, to serve

Preheat the oven to 220°C (425°F), Gas Mark 7 and line a 23cm diameter baking tin with a removable base with baking parchment.

Pulse together the flour, sugar, butter, vanilla extract and baking powder in a food processor, adding 1–2 tablespoons of cold water until it forms a dough. Press the dough into the prepared baking tin and pop in the fridge to rest for 30 minutes.

Mix together the raspberries and crème fraîche in a bowl and then spread them over the base of the pie. Bake in the oven for 15 minutes, then lower the heat to 150°C (300°F), Gas Mark 2 and bake for a further 15 minutes until the pastry is cooked through and lightly golden. Allow to cool, decorate with raspberries and mint sprigs and serve slices with vanilla ice cream.

An epic fruity summer dessert, which can easily be prepared ahead of time and assembled just before you are ready to serve.

SUMMER BERRY & PISTACHIO PAVLOVA STACK CAKE

SERVES 8 (V)

250g icing sugar

4 egg whites

2 tsp cornflour

1 tsp white wine vinegar

500ml double cream, whipped

250g mixed berries

100g pistachio nuts, shelled and finely chopped

Small handful of mint sprigs, to decorate

Preheat the oven to 150°C (300°F), Gas Mark 2. Line two baking trays with baking parchment and draw a large 25cm diameter circle on each piece of baking parchment.

Put the icing sugar and egg whites into a standing food mixer (or use an electric hand-held mixer in a bowl) and whisk on high for 10 minutes until glossy white peaks form. Using a spatula, gently fold in the cornflour and the white wine vinegar.

Divide the meringue mixture between the two baking trays and, using a tablespoon, form two large meringue discs. Bake for 45 minutes, then allow the meringues to cool in the oven.

Assemble the pavlova by spooning half the cream onto the first layer of meringue, then adding half the berries and topping with the other meringue layer, remaining cream and berries. Lastly, sprinkle over the pistachio nuts and decorate with the mint sprigs.

These little rhubarb macaroon bars are a super way to use up those wonderful pink stalks when they appear in early spring. The rhubarb jam filling can also be stored in jars in the fridge and used as a sweet spread on toast.

RHUBARB MACAROON BARS

MAKES 20 BARS (V)
Sunflower oil, for greasing
225g butter, softened
150g caster sugar
2 large eggs
350g plain flour
1 tsp baking powder
3 tbsp milk

FOR THE RHUBARB FILLING
Juice of 1 large orange
175g caster sugar
600g rhubarb, cut into 3cm chunks

FOR THE MACAROON TOPPING
110g butter, softened
75g caster sugar
2 large eggs
1 tsp vanilla extract
275g desiccated coconut
40g plain flour
1 tsp baking powder

Preheat the oven to 180°C (350°F), Gas Mark 4 and grease and line a 20 x 30cm baking tin with baking parchment.

Beat the butter and sugar in a bowl until they are light and fluffy. Add the eggs and beat to combine completely. Using a spatula, fold through the flour and baking powder, then, if necessary, loosen the mixture with the milk.

Transfer the thick batter to the prepared tin and bake in the oven on the middle shelf for 20 minutes until golden brown. Transfer to a wire rack and allow to cool.

While the base is cooking, prepare the rhubarb filling by bringing the orange juice and sugar to a steady simmer in a large saucepan over a medium-high heat. Add the rhubarb and cook the mixture gently for about 20 minutes until the rhubarb has completely broken down and you are left with a thick jam. Turn off the heat and set aside to cool slightly before spreading over the cooked base.

Make the macaroon topping by beating the butter and sugar in a bowl until they are light and fluffy. Add the eggs, one at a time, beating well after each addition. Using a spatula, fold through the vanilla extract, coconut, flour and baking powder. Dot lumps of the macaroon topping roughly all over the rhubarb jam to cover it completely. Return the tin to the oven to cook for 20 minutes until the top is just golden and crisp.

Allow the mixture to cool completely on a wire rack in the tin before slicing into bars.

One of my favourite films is the French classic, *Amélie*. Whenever I make crème brûlée I instantly think of the scene where the heroine catalogues her favourite things, one of them being cracking the crisp caramelised sugar topping of a crème brûlée to reveal the luscious and creamy custard underneath.

CRÈME BRÛLÉE

MAKES 6 (V)

600ml double cream
1 vanilla pod
6 large egg yolks
75g caster sugar
2 tbsp demerara sugar

Preheat the oven to 150°C (300°F), Gas Mark 2. Place six 125ml ramekins in a large high-sided baking tin.

Pour the cream into a saucepan and place it over a medium-high heat. Split the vanilla pod in half and scrape out the seeds using a teaspoon. Add the seeds and the pods to the cream. Bring to the boil and then reduce the heat and simmer for 3–4 minutes.

Add the egg yolks and caster sugar to a large jug and whisk lightly until combined. Remove the vanilla pod from the cream and pour the hot mixture into the egg yolks and sugar, a little at a time and whisking lightly until it is all incorporated.

Pour the mixture into the six ramekins, then pour boiling water into the baking tin until it is just over halfway up the sides of the ramekins. Place in the oven to bake for 40 minutes until the crème brûlées are just set, but still have a little wobble in the middle.

Carefully remove the ramekins from the tin and allow to cool to room temperature. Sprinkle each ramekin with a little demerara sugar and use a blow torch to caramelise the tops (or place the ramekins briefly under the grill preheated to high). Serve straight away.

This makes a wonderfully light and fresh tasting summer dessert and it can easily be made in advance. The pastry is essentially a shortbread mix, which makes a sweet and crumbly base for the tart.

STRAWBERRY CHEESECAKE TART

SERVES 6–8 (V)

FOR THE SHORTBREAD PASTRY

300g plain flour, plus extra for dusting
200g cold butter, diced
100g caster sugar

FOR THE FILLING

100g mascarpone cheese
100g cream cheese
75g caster sugar
Grated zest of 1 lemon
250g strawberries, halved
Mint leaves, to decorate

To make the shortbread pastry, rub the flour and butter together in a bowl with your fingertips until the mixture resembles rough breadcrumbs. Stir through the sugar and 1 tablespoon of cold water until the mix comes together to form a ball. Press it into a flat oval, cover with cling film and place in the fridge to rest for 15 minutes.

Preheat the oven to 180°C (350°F), Gas Mark 4. Dust a clean surface with a little flour and roll out the pastry to 5mm in thickness and large enough to fit a 20cm diameter, 4cm deep fluted tart tin with a removable base. Line the tin with the pastry and press into the sides before trimming the edges.

Prick the base with a fork all over and line with foil, shiny side down, and fill with baking beans. Place the pastry shell in the oven to blind bake for about 15 minutes until the pastry is a light golden brown. Remove the tin from the oven, lift out the beans and foil and allow it to cool on a wire rack.

Meanwhile, beat the mascarpone and cream cheese with the caster sugar and lemon zest (reserving some for decorating) in a bowl until just combined. Make sure not to overbeat. Fill the pastry shell with the cheese mixture and top with the strawberry halves. Decorate with the mint leaves and the reserved lemon zest if you wish. Serve in generous slices.

When my dad was growing up, my granddad took him and his brothers and sisters to Dublin zoo on a cold winter's day. They had brought bags of bananas and monkey nuts to feed the monkeys and were throwing the food over the iced enclosure. One stray banana landed on the ice and suddenly the monkeys realised they could walk across the ice, leading them to charge my granddad and his kids, attacking them for the food. Hence the inspiration for this nutty baked Alaska …

CRAZY MONKEY BROWNIE BAKED ALASKA

SERVES 6–8 (V)

1 litre vanilla ice cream, slightly softened

FOR THE PEANUT BUTTER BROWNIE BASE

150g butter
50g peanut butter
200g dark chocolate (70% cocoa solids), finely chopped
275g caster sugar
3 large eggs
1 tsp vanilla extract
100g plain flour
1 tsp baking powder

FOR THE MERINGUE

6 large egg whites
300g caster sugar

Preheat the oven to 180°C (350°F), Gas Mark 4 and grease and line a 20cm diameter springform tin with baking parchment.

For the peanut butter brownie base, melt the butter, peanut butter and chocolate in a heatproof bowl sitting over a saucepan of simmering water. When melted, remove the bowl from the heat.

In a separate bowl, whisk the sugar and eggs until they are pale and fluffy. Fold through the melted chocolate mixture and the vanilla extract. Sift in the flour and baking powder and fold through. Pour the cake mixture into the prepared tin and bake for about 35 minutes until there is only a slight wobble in the centre. Remove from the oven and set aside on a wire rack until cooled completely. Peel off the baking parchment.

Line a 2 litre (about 16.5cm in diameter) freezerproof bowl with cling film leaving enough to hang over the sides and press the softened ice cream into it. Place the brownie base on top and cover with the cling film overhang. Place in the freezer to firm up for at least 1 hour (although it will last in the freezer for up to a month).

recipe continues…

CRAZY MONKEY
BROWNIE BAKED ALASKA

When you are ready to assemble the baked Alaska, preheat the oven to 240°C (475°F), Gas Mark 9.

To make the meringue, whisk the egg whites in a standing food mixer (or use an electric hand-held mixer in a bowl) and whisk until stiff peaks form. Gradually add the sugar, continuing to whisk until you have soft, silky white peaks. Set aside.

Remove the ice cream and brownie base from the freezer, peel the cling film off the top of the bowl and then turn the ice cream and brownie base out onto a baking sheet, using the cling film to help you.

Peel off the remaining cling film and then spread the meringue mix all over the outside of the brownie and ice cream dome. Place it in the oven to bake for 3 minutes until the meringue is slightly golden. This could also be done with a chef's blow torch. Serve straight away in generous slices.

Lemon meringue pie is just one of those classic show-stopping dessert that is almost always guaranteed to be met with a chorus of oooohs and aaaaahs.

LEMON MERINGUE PIE

SERVES 6–8 (V)

FOR THE PASTRY

200g plain flour, plus extra for dusting
150g cold butter, diced
1 tbsp caster sugar

FOR THE LEMON CURD FILLING

300g caster sugar
100g cornflour
Grated zest of 4 lemons and juice
    of 3–4 (approx. 120ml)
4 large egg yolks
60g butter, diced

FOR THE MERINGUE

4 large egg whites
250g caster sugar
1 tsp vanilla extract

To make the pastry, rub the flour and butter together in a bowl with your fingertips until the mixture resembles rough breadcrumbs. Stir through the caster sugar and 1 tablespoon of ice-cold water until the mix comes together to form a ball. Press it into a flat oval, cover with cling film and place in the fridge to rest for 15 minutes.

While the dough is resting, prepare the lemon curd filling. Place the sugar, cornflour, lemon juice and zest and 450ml of cold water in a large saucepan and whisk to combine. Add the egg yolks and mix throughly.

Place the saucepan over a medium heat and bring the mixture to the boil, stirring continuously until thickened. When it is thick, stir through the butter, then remove the pan from the heat and allow to cool.

Preheat the oven to 180°C (350°F), Gas Mark 4. Dust a work surface with a little flour and roll out the pastry to 3mm in thickness and large enough to fit a 20cm diameter, 4cm deep fluted tart tin with a removable base. Line the tin with the pastry and press it into the sides before trimming the edges.

recipe continues...

LEMON MERINGUE PIE

Prick the base with a fork all over and line with foil, shiny side down, and fill with baking beans. Place the pastry shell in the oven to blind bake for about 15 minutes until the pastry is a light golden brown. Remove the tin from the oven, lift out the beans and foil and allow it to cool on a wire rack.

Put the egg whites in a standing food mixer (or use an electric hand-held mixer in a bowl) and whisk until stiff peaks form. Add a little sugar at a time until it is fully incorporated, then add the remaining sugar and vanilla extract and whisk until just combined.

Place the cooled pastry shell in its tart tin on a baking sheet. Fill with the lemon curd and then spoon the meringue mix on top, piling it high and then using a palette knife to spread it evenly over the top, creating a neat dome. Bake in the oven for about 20 minutes until the meringue is just set and lightly golden. Alternatively, you could skip this baking step and use a blow torch to torch the edges of the meringue until just set.

Leave to cool before transferring to a cake stand. Serve straight to the table.

Semifreddo is an elegant Italian dessert similar to ice cream and can quite easily be made at home. My version uses Nutella and toasted hazelnuts, but you can add ingredients like salted caramel, fruit or nuts.

CHOCOLATE & HAZELNUT SEMIFREDDO

SERVES 6 (V)

100g Nutella

1 large egg

3 large egg yolks

1 tsp vanilla extract

150g caster sugar

400ml double cream

75g toasted skinless hazelnuts, finely chopped

Double line a 1.5 litre capacity loaf tin with cling film. Put the Nutella in a small heatproof bowl and then stand it in a larger bowl of boiling water for 5–10 minutes until it has softened.

Place the egg, egg yolks, vanilla extract and sugar in a heatproof bowl and set it over a saucepan of simmering water. Using a hand-held electric whisk, beat for about 8 minutes until the mixture is thick and pale. Remove from the heat and set aside.

In a separate large bowl, whip the double cream until it is stiff. Fold in the pale egg mixture until combined.

Pour half the mix into the prepared loaf tin. Make a shallow well along the centre and pour in the Nutella. Pour the rest of the semifreddo mix over the top and, using a knife, swirl through the Nutella. Cover with cling film and place in the freezer to set for 6 hours.

To serve, turn the semifreddo out onto a serving platter and carefully remove the cling film. Sprinkle it with the toasted hazelnuts and serve in generous slices.

If you like your sweet treats gooey and chocolatey, then this is the bake for you. A rich chocolate pudding oozing with a layer of salted caramel and a crunchy topping of peanut brittle — what more could you ask for?

SALTED PEANUT CARAMEL MUD PIE

SERVES 8 (V)

FOR THE PEANUT BRITTLE

250g caster sugar

75g salted peanuts, roughly chopped

FOR THE SALTED CARAMEL

150g caster sugar

100ml double cream

½ tsp sea salt

75g butter, diced

FOR THE MUD PIE

225g dark chocolate (70% cocoa
    solids), finely chopped

125g butter, diced

175g caster sugar

1 tsp vanilla extract

100g ground almonds

6 large eggs, separated

To make the peanut brittle, grease a large baking sheet with a little oil. Combine the sugar with 120ml of water in a heavy-based saucepan over a medium-high heat and bring to the boil. Then reduce the heat slightly and allow the mixture to simmer steadily for about 15 minutes, without stirring, until a golden caramel forms. Swirl the pan to encourage the sugar to caramelise.

Remove the pan from the heat and stir through the peanuts. Spread the mixture on the prepared baking sheet and allow to set for 30 minutes. Break up the brittle and bash in a pestle and mortar to a rough crumb. Wash and dry the saucepan ready for the salted caramel.

To make the salted caramel, this time combine the sugar with 50ml of water in a heavy-based saucepan over a medium-high heat and bring to the boil. Then reduce the heat slightly and cook the caramel as for the peanut brittle, making sure not to disturb it until the caramel has formed.

Remove the pan from the heat and pour in the cream and salt and mix through. Don't panic when it bubbles and spits, return the pan to a low heat and the sugar crystals will re-melt. Add the butter and mix through to form a smooth caramel.

Preheat the oven to 180°C (350°F), Gas Mark 4 and line a 20cm diameter springform tin with baking parchment.

recipe continues...

SALTED PEANUT CARAMEL MUD PIE

For the mud pie, melt the chocolate and butter in a large heatproof bowl sitting over a saucepan of barely simmering water.

Remove the bowl from the heat and mix in the sugar, vanilla extract and ground almonds with a spatula. Stir through the egg yolks, one at a time, mixing after each addition, until you have a thick batter.

Put the egg whites in a standing food mixer (or use an electric hand-held mixer in a bowl) and whisk the egg whites until stiff peaks form. Add the egg whites to the chocolate batter and fold through gently until just combined.

Pour two-thirds of the chocolate batter into the prepared cake tin. Using a spoon, pour over the caramel in an even layer, then cover with the remaining batter and place the tin in the oven to bake for about 35 minutes until it is firm but with a slight wobble. Remove the cake from the oven and allow it to sit on a wire rack to cool in its tin.

Carefully remove the mud pie from the tin and transfer it to a cake stand with a lip to catch the caramel as it oozes out while still a little warm. Sprinkle with the peanut brittle and serve in generous slices.

I remember staying in an old Irish guesthouse when I was growing up where a dessert trolley was rolled around the dining room after dinner and you could pick a dessert of your choice. I could never resist creamy profiteroles smothered in a warm thick chocolate sauce.

PROFITEROLE MOUNTAIN

SERVES 4–6 (V)

FOR THE CHOUX PASTRY

60g salted butter
80g plain flour, sifted
3 large eggs

FOR THE CRÈME PÂTISSIÈRE

1 vanilla pod
450ml milk
120g caster sugar
50g cornflour
6 large egg yolks
1 tbsp butter

FOR THE CHOCOLATE SAUCE

60ml single cream
30g caster sugar
50g dark chocolate (70% cocoa solids),
   finely chopped

Preheat the oven 220°C (425°F), Gas Mark 7 and line two large baking sheets with baking parchment.

Place the butter in a saucepan with 130ml water and bring to a steady boil until the butter has melted. Remove the pan from the heat and add the flour, beating with a wooden spoon until a dough comes together. Place the pan back over the heat and beat the dough in the saucepan for about 40 seconds. Remove from the heat once again and set aside. Beat one of the eggs in a small bowl.

Add the remaining two eggs to the warm dough, one at a time, beating thoroughly until completely incorporated after each addition. Add a little of the beaten egg at a time until you have a consistency that will hold its shape when piped. It should be smooth, shiny and just about falling from the spoon.

Using a spatula, scoop the dough into a large piping bag fitted with a large round piping nozzle and pipe small swirls of dough on the lined baking sheets, leaving about 4cm between each swirl to allow for spreading. Brush each one with the leftover beaten egg.

Place in the oven, reducing the heat to 190°C (375°F), Gas Mark 5, for about 15–20 minutes until the choux pastry balls have risen and are golden and crisp. Transfer to a wire rack and use a sharp pointed knife to pierce holes on the underside of the buns. Allow to cool completely before filling.

recipe continues…

PROFITEROLE MOUNTAIN

For the crème pâtissière, split the vanilla pod in half
and scrape out the seeds using a teaspoon. Put both
the seeds and the pod in a saucepan together with the
milk and place over a medium-high heat. Bring to
the boil and then turn off the heat and scoop out the
vanilla pod.

While the milk is coming to the boil, place the sugar,
cornflour and egg yolks in a large mixing bowl and beat
with a whisk until they are thick and pale. Pour the hot
milk into the bowl, whisking quickly and continuously
until it is smooth and incorporated. Pour the mixture
back into the saucepan and place over a medium heat,
beating continuously until it has thickened.

Transfer the crème pâtissière to a cold bowl, flatten the
surface with the back of a spatula and wipe the top
with the butter to prevent a skin forming. Place a piece
of cling film on the surface of the crème pâtissière and
leave it to cool completely.

To assemble the profiteroles, scoop the crème pâtissière
into a piping bag fitted with a small round nozzle and
pipe it into the holes on the underside of the choux buns.

To make the chocolate sauce, put the cream and sugar
into a small saucepan and simmer gently until the
sugar is dissolved. Take off the heat and stir through
the chocolate until it has melted and the sauce is silky
and smooth.

Pile the profiteroles onto a serving plate and drizzle
over the chocolate sauce and decorate if you wish.
Serve straight away.

There is something quite magical about making marshmallows at home.
This version uses strawberry jam to make colourful swirls throughout the
squishy marshmallows.

STRAWBERRY SWIRL MARSHMALLOWS

MAKES ABOUT 36 MARSHMALLOWS

Sunflower oil, for greasing

30g icing sugar

30g cornflour

9 sheets of gelatin

2 large egg whites

450g caster sugar

1 tbsp liquid glucose

100g strawberry jam, strained
through a sieve

Grease a 20cm square baking tin with sunflower oil.
Place a fine sieve on a small plate and add the icing
sugar and cornflour. Use some of the sugar/cornflour
mix to dust the greased tin and set the rest aside.

Place the gelatin and 140ml of cold water in a glass jug
and allow it to sit for 10 minutes.

Meanwhile, put the egg whites in a standing food mixer
and beat until stiff peaks form.

Place the sugar, liquid glucose and 200ml of cold water
in a saucepan. Stir the mixture over a gentle heat until
the sugar crystals have dissolved, then increase the heat
to high and bring it to a steady boil and continue to
cook until the sugar solution reaches 127°C/260°F on a
sugar thermometer. Remove the pan from the heat and
pour in the gelatin mix from the jug. Be careful, as the
mix will bubble dramatically.

Turn the whisk back on and gently trickle in the gelatin
mixture and continue to whisk for 10 minutes until
the mixture turns shiny and thick enough to hold its
shape on the whisk. Pour the marshmallow mix into the
prepared tin and then swirl through the strawberry jam.
Dust with a little of the icing sugar and cornflour and
set aside to cool for at least 1 hour.

Dust a clean surface with more of the icing sugar
and cornflour and turn out the marshmallow slab.
Using a sharp, dusted knife, cut the slab into about
36 marshmallow squares. Coat the exposed edges with
the remaining dusting powder and then serve as a
special treat or pop into an airtight container for later.

It's hard to visit Vietnam without trying Vietnamese coffee. Made by pouring boiling water through individual coffee filters mixed with sweetened condensed milk and served hot or poured over big glasses of ice it can become totally addictive. This sweet coffee flavour works beautifully in this simple no-churn ice cream.

VIETNAMESE COFFEE ICE CREAM

MAKES 1.2 LITRES (V)
600ml double cream
397g tin of condensed milk
60ml strong black coffee
   (Vietnamese if you can find it)
1 tsp vanilla extract

Place all the ingredients in a standing food mixer and whisk on high until soft peaks form. Transfer to a container and freeze for at least 12 hours.

Using an ice-cream scoop dipped in boiling water, serve the ice cream in generous scoops.

There are so many different versions of rocky road and although they are all tooth-rottingly sweet, you can add lots of things like nuts or raisins to pretend you are making them a little healthier. I use condensed milk here to achieve a silky finish to these rich chocolate squares.

MY ULTIMATE ROCKY ROAD

MAKES 12 SQUARES (V)

30g butter, plus extra for greasing
100g condensed milk
200g dark chocolate (70% cocoa solids), finely chopped
200g white chocolate, chopped
100g dried cherries
100g digestive biscuits, roughly crushed
200g mini-marshmallows
Grated zest of 1 small orange (optional)

Grease and line a 20cm square baking tin with baking parchment. Save any baking parchment off-cuts.

In a large saucepan, melt the butter with the condensed milk. At the same time, melt the dark chocolate and half the white chocolate in separate bowls sitting over saucepans of barely simmering water.

To the butter and condensed milk, add the cherries, remaining white chocolate, biscuits, mini-marshmallows and orange zest, if using. Pour over the melted dark chocolate and stir with a wooden spoon until combined.

Tumble the mix out into the prepared baking tin and press down using the baking parchment off-cuts. Drizzle with the melted white chocolate diagonally across the tray. Cover and allow to set in the fridge for 1–2 hours. Cut into 12 pieces.

BAKING DAYS

This fragrant and moist cake is not only visually beautiful, it also has the most delicious spiced sweet orange and honey flavour. The cake can be made gluten-free as long as you use a gluten-free baking powder.

ORANGE POLENTA CAKE WITH HONEY & ROSEWATER SYRUP

SERVES 6–8 (V)

Butter, for greasing

8 green cardamom pods

225g ground almonds

100g polenta

1 heaped tsp baking powder

225g caster sugar

225g butter, softened

3 large eggs

Grated zest of 3 large oranges

1 tsp vanilla extract

50g pistachio nuts, roughly chopped

Crème fraîche, to serve

FOR THE SYRUP

Juice of 2 large oranges

3 tbsp honey

2 tsp rosewater

Preheat the oven to 180°C (350°F), Gas Mark 4 and grease a 20cm diameter springform tin, then line the base with baking parchment.

Bash the cardamom pods in a pestle and mortar and extract the seeds. Then bash the seeds to a fine powder and add to a bowl together with the ground almonds, polenta and baking powder.

Beat the sugar and butter in a bowl until the mixture is light and pale. Add the eggs, one at a time, beating well after each addition. Tip the bowl of dry ingredients into this mixture and fold with a spatula until just combined. Add two-thirds of the orange zest together with the vanilla extract, and just fold through.

Pour the mixture into the prepared tin and place it on the middle shelf of the oven to bake for about 40 minutes or until a skewer comes out clean. Remove from the oven and the tin and allow to cool on a wire rack.

Prepare the syrup by placing all the ingredients in a small saucepan over a medium heat and bringing to a steady simmer.

Pierce holes all over the cake with a wooden skewer while it is cooling and pour over half the syrup, a little at a time, until the cake has soaked it up. Sprinkle with the pistachio nuts, drizzle with the remaining syrup and sprinkle with remaining orange zest to decorate. Serve in slices with a little crème fraîche.

Bagels are surprisingly easy to make at home. It's the same process as making bread, except you boil the bagel shaped dough, which creates a unqiue chewy texture. You can play around with the flavours, made plain, sprinkled with sesame seeds or poppy seeds, they are delicious.

IRISH CHEDDAR & CARAMELISED ONION BAGELS

MAKES 12 BAGELS (V)
(IF USING VEGETARIAN CHEESE)

500g strong white flour, plus extra
   for dusting
1 tsp salt
350ml lukewarm water
7g sachet of easy blend dried yeast
1 tsp caster sugar
1 egg, beaten

FOR THE TOPPING

1 tbsp olive oil
4 large red onions, peeled, halved and
   sliced in half moons
150g Cheddar cheese, finely grated

Combine the flour and salt in a large bowl and make a well in the centre with the back of a wooden spoon. Pour the water, yeast and sugar into the well and allow to sit for 6–8 minutes or until it becomes thick and frothy. Using a wooden spoon, slowly incorporate the flour into the yeast and water mix until you form a dough.

Turn the dough out onto a floured work surface and knead for 6–8 minutes until it becomes smooth and elastic. Grease the mixing bowl with a little olive oil, form the dough into a smooth ball and put it in the bowl. Cover with cling film and a damp cloth. Leave in a warm place to rise for about 45 minutes until the dough has doubled in size.

For the topping, heat the oil in a large frying pan over a medium-high heat. Add the onions and fry gently for about 10 minutes until they are tender and caramelised. Set aside to cool completely.

When the dough has risen, punch it down and turn out onto a floured work surface. With your hands, shape the dough into a long sausage shape and cut it into

12 pieces. Poke your finger through the middle of each piece and form the bagel shape. Place the bagels on two baking sheets lined with silicone mats, cover with cling film and set aside for 20 minutes.

Preheat the oven to 190°C (375°F), Gas Mark 5. Bring a large pot of water to the boil, then reduce the heat so the water is simmering and lower in four bagels at a time. Cook them for about 1 minute on either side, turning with a slotted spoon. Drain the bagels and place back on the baking sheets. Brush with a little beaten egg and place in the oven for 20–25 minutes until they are golden.

Halfway through the cooking time, add a little caramelised onion and cheese to the top of each bagel.

The bagels are great eaten on their own and also make a great base for any sandwich.

This recipe makes a moist coffee swirl cake cooked in a bundt tin. If you don't have one, you can easily make it in a springform tin, buttered and the base lined with baking parchment.

IRISH CAMP COFFEE CAKE

SERVES 6–8 (V)

255g butter, softened, plus extra
    for greasing
340g caster sugar
6 large eggs
240ml milk
120ml sour cream
370g plain flour, plus extra for dusting
1 tsp baking powder
2 tbsp Camp Coffee essence

FOR THE ICING

150g icing sugar
1–2 tbsp water
2 tbsp Camp Coffee essence

Grease a 22cm diameter, 2 litre bundt tin and dust it lightly with flour. Preheat the oven to 180°C (350°F), Gas Mark 4.

Beat together the butter and sugar in a large bowl until the mixture is light and pale. Add the eggs, one at a time, beating well after each addition until they are all combined. Mix through the milk and sour cream, then sift in the flour and baking powder and fold through until you have a smooth cake batter. Pour two-thirds of the mixture into the prepared tin.

Mix the coffee essence into the remaining batter. Drop tablespoonfuls of the mixture into the batter in the tin and use a knife to marble the mixtures together. Place in the oven to bake for about 55 minutes until a skewer inserted into the cake comes out clean. Transfer to a wire rack to cool slightly before removing the cake from the tin. Allow it to cool completely.

For the icing, whisk together the ingredients in a bowl until smooth and then drizzle it over the cooled cake. Serve in generous slices.

Biscotti are one of the easiest biscuits to make at home and also make wonderful edible gifts. These chocolate pistachio biscotti are a great accompaniment to coffee, but you could also try mixing up the ingredients with combinations like white chocolate and almond or sweet cherry and hazelnut.

CHOCOLATE PISTACHIO ESPRESSO BISCOTTI

MAKES 18 BISCOTTI (V)

150g plain flour, plus extra for dusting

50g cocoa powder

1 tbsp instant espresso powder

1 tsp baking powder

100g caster sugar

Good pinch of sea salt

2 large eggs, lightly beaten

2 tsp vanilla extract

50g pistachio nuts, roughly chopped

100g dark chocolate (70% cocoa solids), roughly chopped

Preheat the oven to 180°C (350°F), Gas Mark 4 and line a baking tray with baking parchment.

Combine the flour, cocoa powder, espresso powder, baking powder, sugar and salt in a large mixing bowl. Make a well in the dry ingredients and then add the eggs and vanilla extract and mix together to form a dough.

Turn the dough out onto a floured work surface and then fold and knead the nuts and chocolate into the mix until thoroughly incorporated. Shape into a 21cm by 10cm diameter log, place it on the baking tray and pop in the oven for about 25 minutes until the dough is puffed up and has spread. Remove the tray from the oven and allow the log to cool slightly and harden. Keep the oven switched on.

Carefully cut slices about 1cm thick with a serrated knife and then place the slices back on the baking tray and pop back in the oven to cook for a further 15 minutes until crisp, turning them over halfway through.

Remove the tray from the oven and place the biscotti on a wire rack to cool completely. Store in an airtight container and serve with cups of coffee.

When I was growing up, if Mikado biscuits were in the house, they didn't last long. This cake is a small homage to them with a light sponge layered with jam, covered with a sweet marshmallow frosting and decorated with desiccated coconut.

MIKADO COCONUT CREAM CAKE

SERVES 12 (V)

Butter, for greasing
4 large eggs
170g caster sugar
120g plain flour
½ tsp baking powder

FOR THE FILLING AND FROSTING

340g strawberry jam, strained
   through a sieve
4 large egg whites
225g caster sugar
½ tsp vanilla extract
½ tsp cream of tartar
50g desiccated coconut

Preheat the oven to 180°C (350°F), Gas Mark 4 and grease and line a 20cm diameter springform tin with baking parchment.

To make the sponge, beat together the eggs and sugar until they are pale and fluffy. Sift the flour and baking powder into the bowl and fold gently into the egg mixture, until you are left with no lumps. Pour the mixture into the prepared tin and bake on the middle shelf for about 20 minutes or until a skewer inserted into the centre of the cake comes out clean. Leave the cake to cool slightly in the tin and then turn it out onto a wire rack.

When the cake is completely cool, use a bread knife to divide the cake into two even layers. Sandwich the layers with the strawberry jam, reserving a couple of tablespoons for the top and set aside on a cake stand.

To make the frosting, place the egg whites, sugar, vanilla extract and cream of tartar in a large heatproof bowl sitting over a pan of gently simmering water. Using a hand-held electric whisk, beat on low until the sugar has dissolved completely (check with the back of a spoon against the bowl). Remove the bowl from the heat and continue to beat for 6 minutes until the mixture has transformed into soft and glossy peaks.

Fill a piping bag fitted with a 3mm nozzle with half the marshmallow frosting and then use a palette knife to spread the remaining mixture all over the cake. Pipe the other half of the frosting in two rows all around the outer edge of the top of the cake and then carefully spread a little jam into a disc shape on the centre of the cake. Sprinkle the outer edge of the jam disc with coconut and then gently press the remaining coconut up the side of the cake.

These little muffins are great fun to make as they involve lots of little balls of dough. The dough balls are dipped in butter and then rolled in a cinnamon sugar before being popped into muffins cases to be baked in the oven, resulting in warm sweet muffins.

BUBBLE BREAD CINNAMON MUFFINS

MAKES 10 MUFFINS (V)

375g plain flour, plus extra for dusting

7g sachet of easy blend dried yeast

50g caster sugar

Good pinch of salt

50g butter

200ml milk

75g icing sugar

50g pecans, roughly chopped,
    to decorate

FOR THE COATING

125g butter, melted

125g caster sugar

2 tbsp ground cinnamon

Line a muffin tin with ten paper cases.

Place the flour in a large mixing bowl and mix through the yeast, caster sugar and salt. Melt the butter gently in a saucepan on a low heat. Add the milk and remove the pan from the heat and pour it into the flour. Using a wooden spoon, gently mix the wet and dry ingredients until you have a rough dough.

When the dough has taken shape and is no longer sticky, turn it out on to a floured work surface and knead for about 6 minutes. Form the dough into a smooth ball and return it to the bowl. Cover with cling film and a damp cloth. Leave in a warm place to rise for about 50 minutes until the dough has doubled in size.

Preheat the oven to 180°C (350°F), Gas Mark 4. When the dough has risen, punch it down and split it in two and then roll both pieces into long thin sausage shapes. Cut into 70 evenly-sized pieces, roll in your palms to make small balls and set aside.

For the coating, place the melted butter in one bowl and toss the caster sugar and cinnamon in another. Dip the dough balls in the melted butter and then toss them in the sugar mix to coat. Fill each muffin case with seven balls and bake in the oven for 20–25 minutes or until they rise and turn golden brown.

While they are baking, mix the icing sugar with 2 tablespoons of water until the mixture is smooth and runny. Transfer the icing to a piping bag fitted with a tiny nozzle or use a teaspoon to drizzle.

Remove the muffins from the oven and allow to cool before transferring them to a wire rack and allow to cool completely. Pipe over the icing or drizzle with a teaspoon and sprinkle with the pecans, to decorate.

A visit to NYC is not complete without a visit to the Doughnut Plant, a truly exciting doughnut shop that has the most fantastic collection of doughnut flavours. These crème brûlée doughnuts are inspired by them and are great fun to make at home. To make the caramelised sugar on top it is best to use a small blow torch, which can be bought in most kitchen shops or you could place the doughnut under a very hot grill.

CRÈME BRÛLÉE DOUGHNUTS

MAKES 12 DOUGHNUTS (V)

550g plain flour, plus extra for dusting

50g caster sugar

2 x 7g sachets of easy blend
   dried yeast

125ml milk

2 large eggs

50g butter, melted

Sunflower oil, for frying

200g demerara sugar

FOR THE CUSTARD FILLING

175ml milk

50g caster sugar

3 large egg yolks

1 tbsp cornflour

1 tbsp butter

To make the doughnuts, place the flour, caster sugar and yeast in a large mixing bowl and make a well in the centre. Add the milk, eggs and butter to the bowl together with 100ml of water and, using your hands or a wooden spoon, combine the ingredients until you have a dough. It is a little sticky to work with, but you can add some extra flour if you need.

Turn the dough out onto a floured work surface and knead for 8–10 minutes until it becomes smooth and elastic. Form the dough into a smooth ball and place it back in the bowl. Cover with cling film and a damp cloth. Leave in a warm place to rise for about 50 minutes until the dough has doubled in size.

Meanwhile, prepare the custard filling. Place the milk in a saucepan and gently heat until it just boiling, then remove from the heat. Whisk the caster sugar and egg yolks in a bowl until they are pale and then mix through the cornflour. Slowly pour the hot milk into the egg mixture, whisking until it is all incorporated.

recipe continues...

CRÈME BRÛLÉE DOUGHNUTS

Pour the mixture back into the saucepan and simmer over a low heat, whisking until thickened. Remove from the heat and rub the top with a little butter to prevent a skin forming, allow to cool and cover with cling film. Firm up in the fridge.

When the dough has risen, punch it down and divide into 12 equal pieces and shape into balls. Transfer them to a baking tray dusted with a little flour, cover with a damp cloth and leave to rise again for 30 minutes.

Cook the doughnuts in batches in a deep-fat fryer or a large saucepan filled with sunflower oil at 180°C/356°F for 2–3 minutes on either side or until golden brown. Drain on a plate lined with kitchen paper.

Transfer the custard to a piping bag fitted with a plain 5mm nozzle and inject it into the side of each doughnut. Place the demerara sugar in a bowl. Brush the top of each doughnut with a little water and press the wet side into the sugar to evenly coat it. Using a blow torch (or by placing the doughnuts under the grill preheated to hot), caramelise the sugar until it is golden. Serve straight away.

Banoffee pie has to be one of my desert island desserts and while I still love the pie version, this cake certainly gives it a run for its money with its moist banana sponge layered with a sweet caramel frosting.

BANOFFEE CAKE

SERVES 8 (V)

3 bananas
4 tbsp crème fraîche
2 tsp vanilla extract
175g butter, plus extra for greasing
350g caster sugar
4 large eggs
350g self-raising flour

FOR THE CARAMEL SAUCE

150g caster sugar
100ml double cream
75g butter, diced

FOR THE CARAMEL FROSTING

125g cold butter
375g icing sugar
4 tbsp milk
1 tsp vanilla extract

To make the caramel sauce, combine the caster sugar with 50ml of water in a heavy-based saucepan over a medium-high heat and bring to the boil. Then reduce the heat slightly and allow the mixture to simmer steadily for about 12 minutes, without stirring, until a golden caramel forms. Swirl the pan to encourage the sugar to caramelise.

Remove the pan from the heat and pour in the cream and mix through. Stir in the butter to form a smooth caramel and then set aside.

Preheat the oven to 180°C (350°F), Gas Mark 4. Grease and line two 20cm diameter springform tins with baking parchment.

To make the cake batter, mash two of the bananas in a bowl, then mix in the crème fraîche and vanilla extract. In a separate bowl, cream the butter and caster sugar together until they are light and fluffy. Add the eggs, one at a time, beating well after each addition.

Fold through the flour and banana mixture alternately, then divide the cake batter between the two prepared tins and bake in the oven for about 35 minutes until a skewer inserted in the centre of the cake comes out clean.

recipe continues…

BANOFFEE CAKE

Transfer the tins to a wire rack to cool before removing the cakes from the tins and leaving to cool completely.

Prepare the frosting by beating the butter and icing sugar until smooth, then adding the milk and beating again until smooth. Mix through the vanilla extract and 80ml of the caramel sauce.

Place one layer of the cake on a cake stand and spread half of the frosting on top. Place the second layer over the frosting and use the remaining frosting to completely cover the top. Decorate the top with the remaining banana, cut into slices, and pour over the rest of the caramel sauce, allowing it to drip down the sides. Serve straight away in generous slices.

As my obsession with salted caramel continues to grow, I am being forced to find new socially acceptable ways of eating it — two fingers in the jar just doesn't cut it any more. Enjoyed through the medium of chocolate shortbread biscuits they make an impressive little bake.

SALTED CARAMEL BISCUITS

MAKES 20 BISCUITS (V)

250g butter, softened

250g caster sugar

350g plain flour, plus extra for dusting

125g cocoa powder

2 tbsp cold water

1 tsp vanilla extract

FOR THE FILLING

100g dark soft brown sugar

50g butter

2 tbsp golden syrup

75ml double cream

Pinch of sea salt

Preheat the oven to 180°C (350°F), Gas Mark 4 and line two baking sheets with baking parchment.

In a bowl, beat together the butter and sugar until combined. Sift in half the flour and cocoa powder and add in the vanilla extract. Fold through with a spatula until combined. Then fold through the remaining flour and cocoa powder. When the mixture resembles rough breadcrumbs, stir through 2 tablespoons of cold water and press it into a flat oval shape, cover with cling film and place in the fridge to rest for 20 minutes.

On a floured work surface, roll out the dough to a thickness of 3mm, then use a 6.5cm diameter cookie cutter with a fluted edge to cut out 40 biscuits. Using a small 3.5cm star-shaped cutter, cut out 20 more biscuits. You can also bake the star cut-outs.

Place all the biscuits on the prepared baking sheets and bake in the oven for 12–15 minutes until cooked through. Remove from the oven and allow to cool slightly before transferring to a wire rack to cool completely.

While the cookies are cooking prepare the filling by putting the sugar, butter and golden syrup in a heavy-based saucepan and gently heating to a steady simmer. Continue to cook the mixture until the sugar has been dissolved for 3 minutes. Pour in the cream and sea salt and continue to cook, stirring continuously, for 3 minutes. Transfer to a bowl and allow the sauce to cool completely in the fridge until it is thick and spreadable. Sandwich the round cookies together with a teaspoon of the caramel and serve.

A basic bread recipe should be in the armoury of any self-respecting home cook. It can be adapted to include both sweet and savoury ingredients or be used simply for sandwiches or toast. I like to sprinkle mine with poppy seeds, sesame seeds or rolled oats.

BASIC BREAD RECIPE

MAKES 1 LOAF (V)

450g strong white flour, plus extra
    for dusting
2 x 7g sachets of easy blend dried yeast
1 tsp salt
250ml lukewarm water
1 tbsp olive oil, plus a little extra
1 tbsp honey

SUGGESTED TOPPINGS (OPTIONAL)

1 tbsp poppy seeds
1 tbsp sesame seeds
1 tbsp rolled oats

Combine the flour, yeast and salt in a large mixing bowl and make a well in the centre with the back of a wooden spoon. Whisk together the warm water, olive oil and honey and pour this into the well. Slowly combine the dry ingredients with the water and honey until you have a rough dough.

Turn the dough out onto a floured work surface and knead for 6–8 minutes until it becomes smooth and elastic. Grease the mixing bowl with a little olive oil, form the dough into a smooth ball and put it in the bowl. Cover with cling film and a damp cloth. Leave in a warm place to rise for about 50 minutes until the dough has doubled in size.

Preheat the oven to 180°C (350°F), Gas Mark 4 and dust a 1 litre loaf tin with flour.

When the dough has risen, punch it down and form it into a rugby ball shape, then pop it into the prepared tin. Brush with a little oil and sprinkle with poppy seeds, sesame seeds or rolled oats, if using, and, with a sharp blade, cut three slits across the top.

Bake in the oven on the middle rack for 25–30 minutes until golden brown and the loaf sounds hollow when removed from the tin and tapped. Leave to cool completely on a wire rack before slicing.

The inspiration for this rich, sweet, American pie comes from the movie *The Waitress*. It is ridiculously sweet, but a total treat and perfect for parties.

WAITRESS MERMAID PIE

SERVES 6–8 (V)

75g desiccated coconut

250g digestive biscuits

125g butter, melted

50g mini-marshmallows

100g dark chocolate (70% cocoa solids), roughly chopped

25g butter

Handful of colourful sprinkles

FOR THE FILLING

250g mini-marshmallows

125ml milk

350ml double cream

100g milk chocolate, finely grated

Preheat the oven to 180°C (350°F), Gas Mark 4.

To make the base of the pie, blitz the coconut and digestive biscuits in a food processor until you are left with crumbs. Melt the butter in a large saucepan and then add the crumbs and mix until everything is thoroughly combined. Press the mixture into the base and sides of a 20cm diameter pie tin. Place in the oven and bake for 12 minutes, then remove the tin from the oven and leave it to cool in its tin on a wire rack.

For the filling, place the marshmallows and milk in a wide saucepan and simmer gently until the marshmallows have melted, stirring continuously. Remove the mixture from the heat and allow it to cool completely.

Pour in the cream and whisk until smooth and thickened, then fold through the chocolate. Spoon the mixture into the cooled pie crust. Decorate the sides with the mini-marshmallows and allow to set, covered, in the fridge for 2 hours or overnight.

Just before you are ready to serve, melt the chocolate and butter in a heatproof bowl set over a saucepan of barely simmering water. Drizzle over the pie and decorate with colourful sprinkles. Serve in generous slices.

Peanut butter fans will know that there is only one thing better then the sweet nutty spread itself and that can only be peanut butter cookies. These oaty peanut butter cookies are sandwiched with a smooth sweetened nutty filling.

PEANUT BUTTER SANDWICH COOKIES

MAKES 20 COOKIES (V)

150g caster sugar
120g light soft brown sugar
50g crunchy peanut butter
175g butter, softened
1 tsp vanilla extract
2 large eggs
200g plain flour
1 tsp bicarbonate of soda
250g rolled oats

FOR THE FILLING

250g crunchy peanut butter
100g butter, softened
150g icing sugar, sifted

Preheat the oven to 180°C (350°F), Gas Mark 4 and line two large baking sheets with baking parchment.

Using a standing food mixer or an electric hand-held mixer, cream the two sugars, peanut butter, butter and vanilla extract in a bowl until they are pale and smooth. Add the eggs, one by one, mixing well after each addition so the mix doesn't split. Little by little, mix in the flour and bicarbonate of soda until they are completely incorporated. Using a spatula, fold through the oats until combined.

Place 40 heaped tablespoons of the mixture on the baking sheets and bake for about 15 minutes until golden brown. You may need to swap the trays halfway through the cooking time to get an even colour on the cookies. Remove the trays from the oven and allow to cool slightly before transferring the cookies to a wire rack to cool completely.

For the filling, beat together the peanut butter, butter and icing sugar in a bowl until blended. Add about a heaped tablespoon of the mixture to the flat side of 20 of the cooled cookies and then sandwich together with the remaining cookies. Enjoy with a glass of milk!

In Sweden and Scandinavia, crisp bread dotted with seeds are eaten with most meals of the day. Making them at home is incredibly easy and, best of all, crisp bread can be stored for months in an airtight container. The Swedes use a kruskavel (a rolling pin with large studs) to roll out their crisp bread, resulting in small dimples all across the surface. A similar effect can be achieved by dotting the surface with a fork.

SWEDISH KNÄCKEBRÖD (CRISP BREAD)

MAKES 36 CRISP BREAD (V)

350g coarse rye flour, plus extra
    for dusting

350g wheat flour

4 tbsp sesame seeds

3 tbsp linseed

2 tbsp caraway seeds

7g sachet of easy blend dried yeast

500ml warm water

1 tsp honey

Pinch of salt

Combine the flours, seeds and yeast in a mixing bowl and make a well in the centre with the back of a wooden spoon.

Measure the warm water and stir through the honey and salt. Pour the water into the well and, using a wooden spoon, slowly incorporate the wet and dry ingredients until you have a rough dough. Turn the dough out onto a floured work surface and knead gently for 3–4 minutes until it becomes smooth. Form the dough into a smooth ball and put it in the bowl. Cover with cling film and a damp cloth. Leave in a warm place to rise for about an hour until the dough has risen slightly.

Preheat the oven to 220°C (425°F), Gas Mark 7. Turn the dough out onto a floured work surface and roll into a long thin sausage and then cut out small ping pong-sized balls. Roll each ball out into 2mm thin lengths on the floured work surface and transfer to baking sheets. The Swedes use a rolling pin with ridges to get a dappled surface (see the recipe introduction, above), but you can do the same by pricking with a fork.

Bake for about 10 minutes, turning halfway through the cooking time. Allow the crisp breads to cool on a wire rack before transferring to an airtight container to store.

INDEX

ACKNOWLEDGMENTS

Firstly a massive thank you to all those who have tried my recipes from previous books and TV shows, there is nothing more rewarding doing this job than hearing that the recipes I write are being used in family kitchens and in people's daily lives.

A massive thank you to Helen Wedgewood, Emma Callery, Lizzy Gray and Anna Valentine, at HarperCollins who all shoved me along when I needed shoving to get this book done and dusted! Also to Moira T Reilly, Tony Perdue, Erin Roy, Orlando Mowbray and Laura Lees at HarperCollins, many thanks for the continuous support.

A big thank you to the highly talented Martin Topping and Lucy Sykes-Thompson, who through the interior and cover designs, together have created something truly beautiful and a book I'm incredibly proud of.

I never stopped laughing the day we shot the cover for this book so a big thank you to food photographer hero Myles New, his assistant Tom and food stylist Annie Hudson for making it such a pleasure and for creating such a great cover.

The beautiful food images throughout this book would not have been possible without the stunning food styling of profiterole queen, Sharon Hearne Smith, a big thank you for all your work and support. Also a thank you must go to the lovely ladies and fellow food bloggers who came and assisted during our shoot days, Nessa Robbins, Imen McDonnell, Kristen Jensen, Caroline Hennessy and Catriona Bolger.

A big thank you also goes to Orla Broderick for testing the recipes and making sure everything worked and to her daughter Emily who posed so wonderfully for our banana pancake recipe.

To Brian Walsh at RTÉ, David Hare at InProduction and Suzanne Weldon at SPAR, a massive thank you for creating the wonderful TV show which accompanies the book and of course to Billy Keady, Reamonn De Brún, Marc Dillon, Mark Boland, Robin Murray, Andrew Cummins, Karen Convery and Olivia Marjoram for all the work put in during our shoot. Also a thank you to the folks at Little Piggy Hire who drove the Kitchen Hero van, Gertrude, all over Ireland, Cathy & Stephen Pearson, Antoinette Reynolds and John Jobling Purser.

To my agents in the UK, Rosemary Scoular at United Agents, and in Ireland, Eavan Kenny at Lisa Richards, for their continuous support.

Thank you, thank you, thank you to Sofie, who has to put up with me on a daily basis, she plans, she manages, she drives and also pulled together the beautiful food props throughout this book. I couldn't do it without you so thank you for all the love and support!

As always, a big thank you to my friends and family who sit down and eat the food and make it all worth cooking!

HarperCollins*Publishers*
77-85 Fulham Palace Road,
Hammersmith, London W6 8JB

www.harpercollins.co.uk

First published by HarperCollins*Publishers* 2013

1 3 5 7 9 10 8 6 4 2

Text and photography © Donal Skehan 2013

Donal Skehan asserts the moral right to be identified
as the author of this work.

A catalogue record of this book is available from the
British Library

ISBN 978-0-00-751828-9

Food stylist: Sharon Hearne Smith
Props stylist: Sofie Larsson

Printed and bound by
South China Printing Co. Ltd